SLAVERY TODAY

Auriana Ojeda, *Book Editor*

Daniel Leone, *President*
Bonnie Szumski, *Publisher*
Scott Barbour, *Managing Editor*
Helen Cothran, *Senior Editor*

GREENHAVEN
PRESS®

San Diego • Detroit • New York • San Francisco • Cleveland
New Haven, Conn. • Waterville, Maine • London • Munich

LIBRARY OF CONGRESS CATALOGING-IN-PUBLICATION DATA

Slavery today / Auriana Ojeda, book editor.
    p. cm. — (At issue)
Includes bibliographical references and index.
ISBN 0-7377-1614-2 (pbk. : alk. paper) —
ISBN 0-7377-1613-4 (lib. bdg. : alk. paper)
    1. Slavery. 2. Slave labor. I. Ojeda, Auriana, 1977– . II. At issue (San Diego, Calif.)
HT871.S55 2004
306.3'62—dc21
                                                        2003051617

Printed in the United States of America

Contents

Introduction

In 1993 Abdul Momen, director of the human rights organization Women and Children International, traveled to Tungipara, Bangladesh, where more than one thousand children had been reported missing. The children's mothers told Momen that the children had left with labor contractors who promised to find them good jobs in the Persian Gulf region. Circulating rumors alleged that the children had been abducted and sold into slavery—the girls stocked brothels in India and Pakistan, and the boys served as camel jockeys (boys who ride camels in races) for rich men's entertainment. After months of investigation, Momen concluded that the rumors were true; the children of Tungipara were slaves.

Many people are unaware that slavery still exists all over the world. From the Middle East to the United States, from Eastern Europe to South America, men, women, and children work in slavery or in slavery-like conditions. Anti-Slavery International, the world's oldest human rights group, claims that there are more than 200 million people in bondage. Indeed, some activists maintain that there are more people enslaved today than ever before.

One of the reasons that the problem is so little recognized is because slavery today bears little resemblance to the familiar images of whips, chains, and slave auctions that characterized slavery in the past. Slavery today involves human trafficking, forced labor, debt bondage, child labor, and forced prostitution. As stated by Charles Jacobs, president of the American Anti-Slavery Group, "Modern slaves can be concubines, camel jockeys, or cane cutters. They might weave carpets, build roads, or clear forests." Although most slaves are no longer sold at public auctions, their lives are no easier than the lives of their predecessors. Indeed, for many slaves, conditions today are more miserable and dangerous than in the past.

The most common form of slavery today is debt bondage or bonded labor. A person enters into debt bondage when his or her labor is demanded as a way to pay back a loan. In India, for example, debts running from $14 to $214 are usually incurred for basic necessities, such as food, medical emergencies, marriage dowries (a long-standing cultural tradition), or funeral expenses. Taking into account the outrageous interest rates, often in excess of 60 percent, and the debtors' meager wages, these loans are difficult, if not impossible, to repay. Moreover, inaccurate bookkeeping on the part of the moneylender ensures that the debtor never pays off the loan. Individuals are then forced to repay loans by working for the moneylender for the rest of their lives and often pass the same debt on to their children and grandchildren. Human rights groups estimate that there are approximately 20 million bonded laborers throughout the world.

Severe poverty and the demand for cheap labor are the driving forces behind bonded labor and other forms of slavery today. In Nepal, for instance, the per capita income is $240. By comparison, the per capita income in the United States is $34,100. According to Anti-Slavery International, "Without land or the benefits of education, the need for cash for daily survival forces people to sell their labor in exchange for a lump sum or a loan." Parents in such poverty-stricken nations are forced to accept money in exchange for their or their children's labor. Unscrupulous manufacturers exploit their desperation to secure inexpensive labor to produce goods that later stock the shelves of western clothing stores, carpet dealers, and chocolate makers.

In an economy increasingly driven by global financial markets, Western merchants seek cheap labor to reduce costs and increase profits. Labor in poverty-stricken nations, particularly slave labor, is significantly less expensive than labor in developed countries. Business owners contract with manufacturers in India, West Africa, and other poor countries to produce inexpensive goods to sell in the United States and other western nations. In India, for example, carpet manufacturers force child slaves to make thousands of handmade carpets that eventually end up in American homes. West African cocoa plantations rely on slave labor to satisfy the world's chocolate cravings. Most westerners are unaware that slave labor produces the bricks, charcoal, jewelry, fireworks, and other items that they purchase on a routine basis.

To be sure, most international businesses that import slave-made products do so mostly through negligence rather than intent. Likewise, most consumers are unaware that they are complicit in perpetuating the practice of slavery. Free the Slaves and other nonprofit organizations contend that the international community must work to inform consumers that many of the products that they buy are made by slaves or have slave-made components. In order to eradicate the problem of slavery, these groups maintain, consumers must become aware of the origins of the everyday products they use and demand that they are not produced by slave labor. To achieve this goal, Free the Slaves set up a global partnership to eradicate slavery based on cooperation between nonprofit organizations, businesses, government agencies, labor groups, and consumers around the world. Through this partnership, Free the Slaves strives to identify where slavery exists, monitor areas where labor practices are in question, verify slave-free production of goods, and provide adequate rehabilitation and training for former slaves, among other endeavors.

Free the Slaves is not the only nongovernmental organization (NGO) struggling to end the problem of slavery. Other NGOs, such as Anti-Slavery International, Amnesty International, and the American Anti-Slavery Group, are bringing slavery to the attention of the world. Among their many efforts, these groups have purchased the freedom of slaves in Sudan and Mauritania and pursued harsher punishments for people caught trafficking in humans. The NGOs have also petitioned the United Nations to take action to stop slavery. In response, the United Nations created the Global Program Against Trafficking in Human Beings (GPAT) in 1999. GPAT's many aims include promoting public awareness of the problem of slavery and human trafficking through public service announcements and other campaigns; training law enforcement officers, prosecutors, and judges to respond effectively to the crime of human trafficking; and advising committees on drafting and revising relevant legislation. In addition, GPAT enacted the Protocol to Prevent, Suppress, and

Punish Trafficking in Persons in 2000. The protocol increases penalties for human traffickers, compels governments to combat slavery within their countries, and strengthens protection for victims of trafficking and forced prostitution. Human rights activists hope that these regulations will challenge governments to recognize the existence of slavery within their borders and take the necessary steps to end the practice.

The United Nations' Universal Declaration of Human Rights of 1948 declared, "No one should be held in slavery or servitude; slavery and the slave trade shall be prohibited in all their forms." Despite international laws against slavery, the practice exists throughout the world and shows no sign of abating. Various forms of slavery and efforts to eradicate it are among the issues discussed in *At Issue: Slavery Today*. Whether the international community will unite to rid the world of the abomination of slavery remains to be seen.

1

Trafficking in Humans Is a Global Issue

Anonymous

The following viewpoint was originally an anonymous editorial printed in the San Francisco Chronicle.

Trafficking in humans is becoming one of the most profitable trades in the world, second only to trafficking in drugs and weapons. Traffickers offer destitute families bogus work or educational opportunities in distant countries and then force the unsuspecting victims into prostitution or make them labor in sweatshops. The victims are required to repay their travel costs to the traffickers—often in excess of $20,000—but their meager wages make repayment impossible, leaving the victims under the permanent control of the traffickers. International trafficking in humans is difficult to control because of the various jurisdictions and laws involved. However, world leaders must combat such human rights violations.

Most Americans have no idea that slavery still exists and sends workers and women into bondage. Yet [in June 2000] the United Nations reported that the traffic in people, now the fastest-growing business of organized crime, is only exceeded by the smuggling of drugs and weapons. Pino Arlacchi, director general of the U.N. Office of Drug Control and Crime Prevention, estimates that some 200 million people may now be in the hands of traffickers.

Widening the gulf

How people are attracted, recruited and exploited is not a mystery. The global economy has lifted many of the world's workers into the middle class. But it has also widened the gulf between the rich and the poor, particularly in Africa, Eastern Europe, Russia, China, Southeast Asia and India. As local economies race to join the global economy, industrial development draws rural peasants into pollution-choked cities.

Regions that suffer flooding or desertification—often the result of giant hydroelectric projects, the destruction of forests and natural disasters—create desperate migrants willing to go anywhere to survive. With the collapse of communism, the transition to market economies has turned millions into casualties of rapid economic change.

What traffickers offer is the promise of salvation. But those who seek a better life have no idea they will end up as virtual slaves—if, that is, they survive the passage. The . . . deaths of 58 Chinese migrants trying to reach Britain [in 2000] is just the latest example of the many people who have died in their attempt to escape grinding poverty.

Make no mistake; this is real slavery. When ships filled with human cargo arrive in the United States, people are sold into sweatshop labor until they are able to repay the debt—sometimes as high as $20,000—they owe for transportation. Meanwhile, they are crammed into company-owned housing and, like sharecroppers in the post-slavery American South, forever in debt to their owners for everything they need. As illegal immigrants, moreover, they have no rights and rarely risk deportation by contacting local officials.

What traffickers offer is the promise of salvation.

The traffic in women and girls, also fueled by the poverty and despair of the dispossessed, often involves prostitution. Traffickers prey upon starving families, particularly in Asia, who are unable to feed or provide a dowry for a daughter. According to a recent CIA report, they buy a female child from unwitting families—for less than the price of a toaster—by promising to educate the child in a distant city. Like workers, the girls are held captive, permanently in debt to their owners. Even when a girl manages to escape, she cannot return to her village and dishonor her family. By then, her best chance is to sell herself as a prostitute.

Within the last decade, more than 30 million women and children have been sold within and from Southeast Asia for sweatshop labor or sexual purposes. In Nepal, a land devastated by ecological and economic catastrophe, thousands of girls have been kidnapped and sold to brothels in India.

Many traffickers also target young women from Russia and Eastern Europe who are lured by promises of marriage or a job in a Western city. In Ukraine and Russia, for example, pimps prey upon teenagers who are released from orphanages at age 16. Selma Gasi, an activist in Bosnia, describes how pimps scour war-devastated villages, pretending to look for maids or baby sitters. Yasmina Dimiskovska of the Union of Women in Macedonia confirms that traffickers routinely bring Russian and Ukranian women through her country on their way to Italy. When they arrive, traffickers seize their passports, sell them to brothels and threaten them with violence. Without money, official identity papers, knowledge of the language or the region, the young women are trapped. Without shelters, they have no place to go. And if they do escape, they are shipped home, where they often face retribution from the men who sent them abroad.

[In 1998], Attorney General Janet Reno created an interagency task force that documented the widespread traffic of women to the United States. In April [2000], a CIA report verified that as many as 50,000 women and children from Asia, Latin America and Eastern Europe are brought to the United States every year under false pretenses.

International awareness also grows. In early June [2000], at the Beijing Plus Five meetings at the United Nations, which assessed the status of women and girls around the globe, U.N. Secretary-General Kofi Annan called trafficking, "A worldwide plague." [Former first lady] Hillary Clinton described how the spread of AIDS is creating a generation of orphans, who are becoming easy targets for those who traffic in children. [In 2000], the British Home Office admitted for the first time that hundreds of women from the former Yugoslavia have been sold into sexual slavery after answering phony job advertisements.

Closer to home, [San Francisco] Bay Area residents recently witnessed a classic case of sexual slavery. Lakireddi Bali Reddy, 62, and his son, Vijay Reddy, owners of the Berkeley restaurant Pasand and a small empire of 1,000 rental units, had been allegedly smuggling young women from India. Only when one of the young women died from carbon dioxide poisoning in November 1999—the result of a faulty heater—did federal officials suspect that Reddy had been trafficking in women.

Although the new slavery evokes universal condemnation, the tangle of current international and domestic laws and overlapping jurisdictions makes it difficult to prosecute slave-runners, even when they are identified. Most traffickers receive light sentences. A federal law that forbids any "sale into involuntary servitude" carries a maximum penalty of 10 years in prison. Yet [in 1999], after 70 Thai laborers were held against their will—and forced to work 20-hour shifts in a sweatshop—seven defendants received sentences of four to seven years. One spent only seven months in prison.

That slavery still exists in the 21st century is an international disgrace. True, the problems that give rise to the new slavery are global. But those who would run for president have a rare opportunity to prove their political leadership by focusing global attention on what the U.N. report calls "the biggest human rights violation in the world."

2

Slavery in the United States Is a Serious Problem

Emma Dorothy Reinhardt

Emma Dorothy Reinhardt is the managing director of the American Anti-Slavery Group, a grassroots organization founded in 1993 to combat slavery around the world.

International slave traders lure poverty-stricken foreigners to the United States with promises of employment and better living conditions. However, once they arrive in America, these impoverished foreigners are forced to work for little or no pay, are beaten, raped, and starved, and are told they or their families will die if they run away. Until recently, slave traders and slave owners who were caught served minimal prison sentences. However, the passage of the Trafficking Victims Protection Act of 2000 strengthened penalties for infractions and increased protections for victims. The new legislation, combined with greater community awareness, may reduce the problem of slavery in the United States.

Beatrice was recruited at age 13 to live with an American family, help with the housework, and attend school. Her parents, hoping she would have a better standard of living and education, agreed.

Upon arrival in the United States, however, Beatrice found herself enslaved: locked in a suburban home, working for up to 20 hours a day, and denied education. Regularly, she was forced to hold her hands above her head and kneel on the floor for long periods while being beaten. In 1998, after she had been beaten for over an hour, her screams alarmed the neighbors. The police were called, and Beatrice was discovered.

She had been held captive in the United States for nine years.

Beatrice is from Nigeria and was enslaved in 1989 in New York by a child-welfare worker and her husband. But Dora is from Ghana; Vasantha from Sri Lanka; Chanti from India; Yua Hao from China. They were all enslaved here over the last two decades. Discovered in Washington, D.C., Boston, Berkeley, California, and Bryant, Arkansas, respectively, these victims were enslaved by a World Bank employee, a Boston University student, a landlord, and a television executive.

Incredibly, slavery has returned to our shores. Forced to work for no pay under the threat of violence, a slave is a human being whose time and body are owned by another. Though legally abolished in 1865 in the United States, slavery has not ended here.

Thousands of Beatrices, Doras, Vasanthas, Chantis, and Yua Haos suffer today in America.

Over 27 million people are slaves in the world. In the United States alone, 50,000 women and children are trafficked every year. Thousands of men also suffer as slaves here, but their cases are rarely in the headlines. Behind barred windows, in swanky upscale apartments, in dim-lit basements, hundreds of thousands—women, children, and men—endure slavery.

Modern-day slavery is one by-product of globalization.

Americans are shocked and disbelieving. Isn't slavery prohibited?

We are familiar with the concept of trafficking, which we associate with smuggling guns and drugs. Strong civil, human, and women's rights campaigns have informed us about domestic violence in this country, which occurs in small towns, major cities, and places in between. We have learned about antebellum slavery and the philosophies that protected and perpetuated the system. We know many slave owners were once viewed as highly respectable and that they made profits from their slaves. And we were taught that slavery continued on even after it was made illegal.

We must now weave these three concepts into the inconceivable: A complex, transnational, and highly profitable slave trade exists today. Slaves are bought and sold in this country, at this time. Cities all over the world act as the points of transfer, sale, and settlement in this international network. The United States is not spared this evil.

Who? How?

Achara lived in a small village in the mountains of northern Thailand. Though they worked hard, her family never had enough food for the family of eight. Sometimes, Achara's mother would tell her children stories of families who worked hard and had plenty.

When Achara was 12, a businessman came to her village and offered her a well-paying restaurant job in New York City. He guaranteed visas, transportation, and enough money to support herself and help her family. He asked for part of the U.S. $50,000 fee up front. Achara's parents saw this as a great opportunity. The extended family raised U.S. $30,000—a sum greater than any villager could earn in a lifetime.

Within one month, Achara had reached her destination. But rather than finding freedom and prosperity, she was ensnared immediately. She was robbed of her documents, thrown into a small room with 16 other young women, and made to work in a nearby restaurant for 12 hours each day. She was told that if she did not show up for work or tried to run away, she would be raped and beaten, and her family back home would be killed.

After the first month, the situation worsened. Her master told Achara that her restaurant work was not enough. She would now be required to have sex with at least 20 men each day to repay her debt.

Achara endured forced labor and forced prostitution for two and a half years. By chance, she learned about a shelter for Asian victims of domestic violence, which helped her to escape. But she is still unsafe. She worries about the safety of her family and fears deportation.

For security reasons, Achara represents a composite of many people who have been enslaved here. And there are many other forms of slavery. Slavery is a truly complex industry and extremely diverse. Both genders and all ages of people have been lured into slavery. There was "Got," a two-year-old boy from Thailand who was used to trick border guards into believing that the man and young woman with whom he traveled were his parents, rather than a smuggler and his victim. He had been sedated and used as a human prop. "Got" was discovered in a Los Angeles airport. . . .

Modern-day slavery is one by-product of globalization: slaves come from Thailand, Brazil, China, India, Ethiopia, Mauritania, Nigeria, Cameroon, Poland, Russia, Brazil, and Mexico.

"While there is not one classic example of slaves in the United States today," explains Carol Gomez, project coordinator for CATW (Coalition Against the Trafficking in Women) and a domestic violence counselor at the Massachusetts General Hospital, "there are common disadvantages. The trafficked individuals often arrive here unable to speak, read, or understand English. Additionally, they may be without documents." While some of those trafficked into this country do not have visas and passports, most individuals did at one time have documentation (though often fraudulent) but were stripped of it upon arrival. Because of this, "the dependency on the abusive smugglers, pimps, traffickers is increased," states Gomez.

Vulnerability underlies the slave industry in the United States and is at the start of the system of enticement in the recruits' home villages. The luring process is systematic and systemic. As in Achara's case, the process usually results in debt bondage. The trafficker keeps the financial records and makes the rules of payback so that the debt accrues interest rapidly.

The slave, paid almost nothing, is barely able to afford her cost of living (paid to the same slaveholder), much less the ever-growing debt. Is this not enough? Slaveholders maintain control of their victims by telling them that escapees will be shot by the man across the street or gang-raped by the policemen on the corner.

Who would do this?

The slaveholders are as varied in profile as the slaves are in cultural origin. Some traffickers fulfill the stereotype of petty gangsters, slinking in dark, underground networks, fronting their illicit enterprises in immigrant communities. But some traffickers are trusted by mainstream communities.

Reddy is a man in his sixties who happens to be one of the wealthiest landlords in Berkeley, California. In February 2000, he was charged with bringing young Indian girls to Berkeley as sex and labor slaves. Porges happens to be one of Manhattan's most successful asylum attorneys. In September 2000 he and his law firm were accused of acting as accomplices in the smuggling and enslavement of 6,000–7,000 Chinese women and men over the last seven years.

Laake Tesfaye, advocate at the Ethiopian Community Development Council in Arlington, Virginia, works with those who are enslaved by employees of international organizations such as the United Nations, the World Bank, and the IMF [International Monetary Fund]. "The employees bring people here and hide them. They must work seven days a week, 12-plus hours each day. They are paid almost nothing—usually about $100 per month," Tesfaye explains. "We have many cases like this. But it is very difficult to even estimate how many cases are in the D.C. area, because most of the servants can't make phone calls, can't leave the house. The only people who report to us are the people who escape."

Tesfaye recalls a recent case in which two young women from Ethiopia escaped from their masters' homes. They had been used as slaves in Saudi Arabia, then transferred to the United States. "An employee from the World Bank just transferred her to a friend, as a gift. They just give them like presents," he reports. "We are negotiating with the World Bank and IMF to strictly supervise and monitor the situation with G5 workers [those working for employees of international organizations]. We are demanding for the servants their basic human rights—pay, food, health care. We just want them to be treated as human beings."

Are the perpetrators punished?

Up until now, slaveholders, when found guilty, have been fined and/or sentenced to limited prison terms. In contrast to those found trafficking in drugs or weapons, however, human traffickers have rarely been given long prison sentences. The ringleader in the Paoletti case, in which over 1,000 deaf and mute Mexicans were forced to hawk trinkets in various U.S. cities, received only 14 years in prison, while his coconspirators received between 1 and 8 years. This reality has appalled experts. "The sentencing guidelines should be sufficiently stringent to reflect the heinous nature of such offenses," says a November 1999 report by the Center for the Study of Intelliegence.

With the recent passage of the Trafficking Victims Protection Act of 2000, however, the penalties may be more severe. "We have a really good piece of legislation to start with," remarks Jennifer Stanger, media and advocacy director of LA-based CAST (Coalition Against Slavery and Trafficking). The act provides legal protection and welfare to the victims. The result will be that fewer escaped slaves will be instantly deported back to their countries of origin. Individuals who suspect a case of slavery will feel safer to report it, without risking reprisals against the family in the home country.

Even with this legislation, the victims' security is not guaranteed. Quynh Dang, program director at the Asian Task Force in Boston, describes the plight of a mail-order bride from Southeast Asia who was brought to the United States by a man in the Boston area. "When she came here, she found out that the man had married her for low-cost domestic help. She was kept in the basement. When it got too warm, she was moved to the garage. A neighbor saw her living in the garage and contacted us.

"She left him," Dang continues. "But he tracked her down. Now she's back with him. She was going to file for divorce. He doesn't allow her to pick up the phone, though, so we have not been able to contact her." It appears that the young woman is trapped again. "Even if she does succeed in divorcing him," Dang explains, "her legal status may still be very insecure. He had promised her a whole lot of things, including legal residency."

Dang states that approximately 5 percent of the task force's 200–230 cases each year can be instantly classified as cases of slavery.

Organizations working with victims of domestic violence, especially in immigrant communities, as well as those providing legal services to individuals seeking asylum, are coming across many cases of slavery. Sarah Ignatius, an immigration attorney at the PAIR (Political Asylum Immigrant Refugee) Project in Boston, remarks that she has "worked with people who have found themselves in slavelike conditions here—situations they have landed in because they were trying to escape another different and unfortunate situation back home."

Ignatius offers, "The new legislation holds some promise. But if they [the victims of involuntary servitude] have just been slaves in the United States, and their slaveholder is from the United States and not likely to persecute them back in their own home country, it is not likely to be an asylum case." Much advocacy and lobbying work surrounding the new legislation is required, as is further domestic and international research.

"As training and awareness increase," Stanger observes, "so will the amount of cases reported through community referrals. And we want to encourage people to prosecute. They [escaped slaves] are entitled to that restitution, and we want to be empowering them to exercise their human rights." Coalitions committed to providing service to those escaping slavery in the United States must be strengthened.

What to do: Americans respond

Many Americans are involved with human, civil, and women's rights organizations. Is the issue of modern-day slavery on their respective agendas?

Recently a representative from an industry that uses unskilled labor called the American Anti-Slavery Group to tell us that he has heard of employers who recruit men from Mexico and then hold them captive while they try to work off their inflated debts. "I want any and all information you have about systems of slavery in this country," he asked.

We need to be aware of those working beside us. Is something peculiar happening in the apartment next door? Who lives there? Is the young woman who works for a colleague rarely seen outside the house? Where do the men who do construction in the neighborhood live? Is the cleaning lady paid directly? Who picks your children's friends up from school?

Americans need to ask themselves these questions—not to incriminate others but to begin to notice others' well-being. We are free. We are aware. We are responsible. We are all guaranteed human rights.

The system of identification, exposure, and emancipation of modern-day slaves in the United States is still in its early stages. Abolitionists today are asked only to be aware. Be vigilant. Be vocal. And teach others to do the same.

3

Slavery in Mauritania Is a Serious Problem

Moctar Teyeb

Moctar Teyeb is the American coordinator for El Hor, a Mauritanian antislavery organization run by former slaves, and serves as the outreach director of the American Anti-Slavery Group, a grassroots organization that works to combat slavery around the world.

In Mauritania, slavery is a long-standing institutionalized social system. Black chattel slavery is thriving in Mauritania, where Arab slave owners (beydannes) control African slaves (haratines) by convincing them that serving their lighter-skinned masters is their religious duty. The international community must acknowledge that slavery exists in Mauritania and strive to abolish the practice.

Slavery is not history. From Bombay to Brazil, at least 27 million people are enslaved around the world, more than ever before. Westerners know about forced prostitution in Thailand and carpet-slave children in Asia, but few know that in my country of Mauritania, black chattel slavery has never ended; hundreds of thousands of slaves live as the inheritable property of their masters. Mauritania is a small nation located on the west coast of Africa, right above Senegal. Of a population of 2.4 million, nearly half are black Muslim slaves. . . . In the year 2000, Mauritania's centuries-old system of slavery remains strong.

Creating a slave caste

Eight centuries ago, my ancestors lived peacefully in their homeland of Africa. Then came the Arab-Berber raids. Suddenly, in the night, under the cover of darkness, Arab-Berber raiding parties from the north descended on our villages. These raiders stormed through on horses and camels. They killed or chased off the men, and took the women and the children away, tied to the backs of their animals. Why women and children? Because they could be controlled and raised to believe that their role as blacks was to serve their new masters. And they could be made

Moctar Teyeb, "A Call for Freedom," *Tikkun*, vol. 15, July 2000, p. 10. Copyright © 2000 by the Institute for Labor and Mental Health. Reproduced by permission of Tikkun: A Bimonthly Jewish Critique of Politics, Culture, and Society.

into a slave caste. In this way, we became haratines—black Muslim slaves who faithfully served our white Arab masters, the beydannes. The system of slavery that began with these raids in the twelfth century continues today. On my mother's side, we cannot remember a time when our family was ever free.

Those of you who know the history of the Middle East and North Africa are aware that before the Trans-Atlantic slave trade, there existed for centuries a Saharan slave trade. Timbuktu, for instance, was well known as a stop on the Saharan caravan route. There were three kinds of goods on those caravans: gold, ivory . . . and black slaves. As a result of those caravans, slavery became an accepted institution in the region in which I was born. Slaves were—and still are—the property of masters; they exist to serve the master's every need. Although officially outlawed by an ordinance enacted in 1981, there is little evidence that this measure has ever been enforced. Moreover, the Islamic courts regularly uphold the rights of slave owners. For the Arabs in Mauritania, it is shameful to work with one's hands. So slaves cook, clean, and wash the hands of the masters before they eat. Slaves haul water, herd cattle, and cultivate land. Slaves are also given as gifts or as loans. When the daughter of a master marries, she must move to the house of her husband's family, along with two slaves to serve her and show her noble status.

The haratine slaves are faithful Muslims, and are raised to believe that serving their master is their religious duty.

Let me make clear that everyone in Mauritania is Muslim—the masters and the slaves. The haratine slaves are faithful Muslims, and are raised to believe that serving their master is their religious duty. Young slaves are told by their owners that because of their impure black skin, their only hope for reward in the afterlife is being obedient. Many slaves grow up believing this and transmit this myth to their children. In Mauritania, we have a simple saying: "Paradise under your master's foot."

A twisted version of Islam

The values and concepts that drive the Mauritanian system of slavery are backed by a twisted version of Islam. The beydannes do not allow black haratines to learn the Holy Koran because, they say, black slaves are too impure for such a holy book. Only the beydannes have the right to learn the Koran, and the hard result is that the slaves are more obedient without knowing the truth of Islam. Masters also deny slaves the right to marry. The masters believe that if haratines make their own marriage, they will begin to feel independent. Therefore, even the most fundamental religious (i.e., Islamic) right of marriage is denied them.

This is all in violation of the Holy Koran. Since I escaped from bondage, I have spent many years studying Islamic law, and I know that God is very clear on the issue. Freeing slaves is a high form of charity. As it is written in the Koran: "The alms are only for the poor and the needy, and are used to free captives and debtors for the cause of Allah, for this is a duty imposed by Allah."

But the beydannes have reversed this concept. When rich masters want to make repentance, they do not "free a neck," as the Koran says. Instead, they give one of their slaves as charity to the poor. So today, you can walk in the capital city of Nouakchot and see blind beggars being led around by their black slaves. Mauritania has many social classes and clans, but all the light-skinned beydannes share the right to enslave blacks.

For hundreds of thousands of blacks in Mauritania, slavery is . . . a brutal reality.

There are no more slave raids. Everyone has enough slaves, and more are obtained by breeding. In addition, there are no open markets for slaves. Trading is done informally, by word of mouth. In the early 1980s, when some princes in the Gulf countries of Qatar and the United Arab Emirates needed slaves, they imported them from Mauritania. Owners in Mauritania would sell young children to sheiks in the Gulf. Inside Mauritania, some masters hire out their slaves to companies in return for salaries, or rent slaves out to other masters in big cities.

In the late 1970s, I joined El Hor, a Mauritanian antislavery group run by former slaves. El Hor means "the Free" (like the Hebrew word for freedom: "herut"). We take our inspiration from runaway African American slaves, like Frederick Douglass, who escaped to become abolitionist leaders and who could not rest until they freed their people. El Hor challenges everyone to visit Mauritania to see how slavery is a part of everyday life, to see how the beydannes in Mauritania consider slavery a religious right they will not give up. You might also look more closely, here in the Mauritanian embassies and consulates in New York and Washington [D.C.]. In these buildings you will find slaves serving the diplomats.

Silence for slaves

Tragically, our brothers in Islam have never condemned the practice of slavery in Mauritania. They have denied and neglected what is happening to us, even though we haratines are proud Muslims. Muslim and African leaders must know that slavery in Mauritania is a reality, and should put pressure on the dictatorship in Mauritania to end slavery.

We are also dismayed at the silence from the human rights community. Human rights groups have known about slavery in Mauritania for years, but have yet to launch a concerted effort to address contemporary slavery. There are so many organizations and humanitarian groups dedicated to fighting child abuse, political detentions, and disasters. But these groups have forgotten about one million slaves in Mauritania. Some do not know. Others do not care. Human Rights Watch, for instance, has no Mauritania desk. The human rights community must remember that the fight against slavery over 150 years ago was the first modern human rights campaign. That fight is no less important today.

Until recently, the U.S. State Department extensively documented slavery in Mauritania. After Mauritania abandoned its support of [Iraqi leader] Saddam Hussein, the State Department rewarded this moderation by citing mere "vestiges" of slavery in its annual human rights reports. In fact, there had been no change whatsoever in Mauritania's official policies on slavery. And despite a 1996 congressional resolution decrying chattel slavery in Mauritania (HR 4036-3), the current administration continues to engage Mauritania as a moderate Arab state. The price of this rapprochement is my people's freedom. In October [1999], Mauritania and Israel signed a peace treaty, further deepening our plight.

For hundreds of thousands of blacks in Mauritania, slavery is no "vestige," it is a brutal reality. But we slaves have rights; although neither our government nor our religious leaders will admit it, we, like all human beings, have the right to freedom. And we are committed to fighting for our rights. Those of us who have escaped do two important things. First, we educate slaves back home that bondage is wrong, because knowledge is the path to freedom. Second, we speak out against Mauritanian slavery. El Hor has called for an international conference to take place in Europe or the United States. It is important for leaders and organizations to begin to address slavery in Mauritania. We must break the silence and begin discussion.

As outreach director of the American Anti-Slavery Group, I have spoken to children and adults at schools and at protest marches. I see students starting antislavery campaigns, and I see adults demanding action. I see that the old spark of abolitionism is once again touching the souls of Americans. This gives me hope because I know that when Americans speak out against human rights abuses (as in Kosovo and South Africa, for example), the American government responds.

Freedom from bondage is the most fundamental human right, and America is a proud abolitionist nation. But your work is not over. After 800 years of bondage, one million black Muslim slaves can no longer be ignored. The rights of black children born into slavery must be protected. The rights of mothers who cannot even claim their own children must also be protected. And the rights of men and women who cannot marry must be protected. I know you will stand with me and my people. And so I say to you, "Next year in a Free Mauritania."

4

Bonded Labor
Enslaves the Poor

Beth Herzfeld

Beth Herzfeld is the press officer for Anti-Slavery International, a non-profit organization dedicated to eliminating slavery around the world.

Bonded labor, one of the most common forms of slavery today, refers to labor that is performed in repayment of a debt. Unfortunately, many people are trapped into bonded labor when their wages are too low to cover the debt's interest rate and principal in addition to living expenses. International organizations, such as the United Nations and Anti-Slavery International, are working toward freeing victims of bonded labor. More support is needed to combat this terrible form of slavery.

We all thought slavery had been abolished, but at least 20 million people are still enslaved in the world today through bonded labour.

Although this is the most widespread form of slavery today, it is also the least known. Most people become bonded when their labour is demanded as a means of repayment for a loan, or for money given in advance. Usually they are forced by necessity or are tricked into taking a loan in order to pay for such basic needs as food, medicine and for social obligations—the costs of a wedding or a funeral. A loan for as little as 30 Pounds [UK] in some countries can take a lifetime to repay. Bonded labourers are typically forced to work long hours regardless of their age or health, sometimes for seven days a week, 365 days a year. They receive food and shelter as "payment", but might never be able to pay off the loan.

Entire families in Nepal, India and Pakistan can be affected by this brutal system, with the debt being handed down through generations. Once the loan is taken, bonded labourers are deprived of their rights to negotiate terms and conditions of work. They have to pay high rates of interest on these loans, and because they do not even receive a minimum wage, the cycle of interest and debt keeps them enslaved.

Trapped in this cycle, bonded labourers find it almost impossible to pay off their debts. Poverty, long hours of hard labour, poor diet and lack of access to health services mean they frequently become ill. Time off

Beth Herzfeld, "Campaigning Against Bonded Labour," *IFWEA Journal*, December 2000. Copyright © 2000 by International Federation of Workers' Education Associations. Reproduced by permission.

work because of sickness and medical treatment only increases the level of debt and perpetuates the cycle of debt bondage.

The current combination of mass migration from poverty and the global demand for sources of cheap, expendable labour has expanded this system beyond India, Pakistan and Nepal where it has existed for centuries. Girls in Benin are sold as maids in Gabon and eastern European women are bonded into prostitution in western Europe. Even though bonded labour is illegal in most countries, it is expanding.

Bonded labourers find it almost impossible to pay off their debts.

In some cases people may not even be aware that a loan has been made. In Brazil, for example, agricultural workers are recruited from areas of high unemployment to work in distant estates. Although they are promised food and transportation, they are not told that the expense of transporting them will be deducted from their salaries. Their debts increase because, in many cases, the estates are isolated and they are dependent on the 'company store' for provisions which are sold at inflated prices.

Migrant domestic workers

In Africa, Asia, Europe and the United States, the enslaving of migrant domestic workers affects both young girls and grown women from the world's poor. They work within their national borders or travel abroad to richer nations. They enter this work with the expectation that their and their family's lives will be materially better than if they stayed at home and found work locally.

Although some manage to secure good jobs, millions unsuspectingly enter lives of servitude characterised by abuse, exploitation, violence, and physical and mental torture. Many work between 10 to 15 hours a day with no or very limited time off for little or no pay.

Because they work in the home, they have no contact with the outside world. There is no possibility for them to negotiate their working conditions, such as hours of work, time off, pay and any other areas of work protected by labour legislation. They are at the complete mercy of their employer.

In many countries, such as in the Gulf States, they are excluded from labour laws altogether because they are regarded as members of the household rather than as independent workers.

In Britain most migrant domestics come from Sri Lanka, India and Nigeria. But the largest number come from the Philippines, usually brought in by temporary residents.

The experience of Alice illustrates how many are tricked into debt bondage. Recruited from Manila for work in Kuwait, Alice was eventually taken by her employers to work for them in London.

> Despite Alice's qualification as a civil engineer in Manila, the pay was not enough to support her and her family. She an-

swered an advert recruiting engineers to Kuwait offering 215 Pounds per month—six times her Philippine salary. Against her expected salary her family borrowed money so she could pay the agency's fee, half of which was due before leaving Manila. Upon arriving in Kuwait City she found that there were no civil engineering posts, only jobs for maids at a salary considerably less than she was promised. With no money to pay the agency or to pay for the flight back home, she had no choice but to sign a contract to work as a domestic.

Her day began at 5:30 A.M. and only ended once all of the adults had gone to bed, which was regularly after 2 A.M. She had no time off, not even to go to church or to write letters home.

After two and a half years in Kuwait Alice was taken to London. Following an attack in which her employer tried to rape her she fled. It was the first time she had been out of the house.

With no money or passport it is difficult for such women to escape. They are kept isolated from people beyond the household and are frequently locked indoors. Even if they do escape, many do not have money and are unfamiliar with the area. Furthermore, they have no papers because the employer keeps their passports.

Individuals in bonded labour are routinely threatened with and subjected to physical and sexual violence.

Individuals in bonded labour are routinely threatened with and subjected to physical and sexual violence. They are kept under various forms of surveillance, sometimes by using armed guards. Even though few cases involve keeping them in chains, the constraints are just as binding. Their lives are under the complete control of those whom they owe money to, to the extent that employers who use bonded labour sometimes sell the debts—and thereby the people—on to others. In Rawalpindi, Pakistan, brick kiln workers tell of being sold more than ten times.

International instruments

The 1948 Universal Declaration of Human Rights, which applies to all members of the United Nations, prohibits the practice of slavery in all of its forms. The UN Supplementary Convention on the Abolition of Slavery, the Slave Trade, and Institutions and Practices Similar to Slavery, which most countries have ratified, and the International Labour Convention No. 29 Concerning Forced or Compulsory Labour, form the key international instruments banning bonded labour. But the lack of political will to enforce these laws and develop or implement domestic legislation perpetuates bonded labour.

Poverty and limited access to education are key to this system's continuation. Without land or the benefits of education, the need for cash for daily survival forces people to sell their labour in exchange for a lump sum or loan.

Crucial to eliminating this form of slavery is the implementation of existing international and domestic legislation which prohibit bonded labour in addition to the creation of alternative sources of income, and credit for those in bonded labour.

By working with inter-governmental bodies such as the United Nations, Anti-Slavery International focuses international attention on governments that have not taken adequate steps to eliminate slavery in their country.

In June [2000], the United Nations Working Group on Contemporary Forms of Slavery met in Geneva. Anti-Slavery's successful lobbying made bonded labour a focus for its 2000 agenda. Working with other activists, we were successful in pressing for the Group's final resolution to include issues key to ending this form of slavery, such as calling for government action against all reported cases of bonded labour, enforcing existing anti-bonded labour laws, and for governments to develop effective programmes preventing freed labourers from returning to this system of debt.

In 2002, information on measures taken by member states to suppress or prevent debt bondage will be submitted to the Group and future sessions will evaluate progress made.

Political will is key. The will for the international community to demonstrate to offending States that breaking international standards is unacceptable. The will for Governments to fulfil their promises codified in law that bonded labour will indeed be ended and that those who are found guilty are penalised.

Anti-Slavery International launched its campaign against bonded labour [in] October [2000]. By getting involved you can do something about it. Join our Campaigns Network and add your voice to our campaign.

5

Slavery Is Big Business

Kevin Bales

Kevin Bales is the director of Free the Slaves, the North American sister organization of Anti-Slavery International, and the author of Disposable People: New Slavery in the Global Economy.

Today's slaves are cheap and disposable, making it easy for owners of brothels, plantations, and factories in developing nations to make huge profits from their labor. These producers sell their goods to businesses in industrialized nations, who then market them to unsuspecting consumers. Unfortunately, few Western businesses are taking action against unscrupulous suppliers. Many businesses contend that it is impossible to control how their products are made, and others maintain that the problem is not their responsibility. However, consumers and activists are becoming more aware of slavery and are pressuring businesses and governments to reduce the practice. As a result, more efforts are being made by the United Nations and antislavery organizations to eradicate slavery.

[In] April [2001], the world's media zoomed in on the 'slave ship' of Benin. The ship, reported to be carrying 200 enslaved children, was refused entry to Gabon and Cameroon. For two days it disappeared while a search was mounted and fears grew over the fate of the children. When the ship finally reappeared and docked in Benin, it had on board only 43 children and 100 or so adults. After questioning, it was found that most of the children were being trafficked to work in Gabon. In spite of this the ship's captain denied any involvement. The Benin Government then suggested that there was another ship with child slaves, but none was located. Were there other child slaves? Was there another ship? At this point no one knows.

What we do know is that this confusing incident is just a small part of the regular human traffic between Benin and Gabon. What was news to the world's media is well known in West Africa—on what was once called the Slave Coast, the trade continues. Increasingly, children are bought and sold within and across national borders, forced into domestic work, work in markets or as cheap farm labour. UNICEF [United Nations International Children's Emergency Fund] estimates there are more than 200,000 children trafficked in West and Central Africa each year.

A significant money-maker

Child slavery is a significant money-maker in countries like Benin and Togo. Destitute parents are tricked into giving their children to slave-traders. A local UNICEF worker explains: 'People come and offer the families money and say that their children will work on plantations and send money home. They give the family a little money, from $15 to $30—and then they never see their children again.'

While a slave ship off the African Coast is shocking at the turn of the 21st century, it represents only a tiny part of the world's slavery which has seen a rapid escalation since 1945 and a dramatic change in character.

Three things have sparked this rapid change. Firstly, the world's population has tripled since 1945 with the bulk of the growth in the Majority World [the developing world]. Secondly, economic change and globalization have driven rural people in poor countries to the cities and into debt. These impoverished and vulnerable people are a bumper crop of potential slaves. Finally, government corruption is essential. When those responsible for law and order can be made to turn a blind eye through bribes, the slave-takers can operate unchecked.

Today's slave is cheap and disposable.

This new slavery is marked by a dramatic shift in the basic economic[s] of exploitation—slaves are cheaper today than at any other time in human history. The agricultural slave that cost $1,000 in Alabama in 1850 ($50,000 at today's prices) can be purchased for around $100 today. This fall in price has altered not only the profits to be made from slavery, but the relationship between slave and master as well. The expensive slave of the past was a protected investment; today's slave is cheap and disposable.

A good example is a 14-year-old girl sold into a working-class brothel in Thailand. Her initial purchase price might be less than $1,000. In the brothel she will be told she must repay four times that to gain her freedom—plus rent, food and medicine costs. Even if she has sex with 10–15 men a night, her debt will keep expanding through false accounting and she will never be allowed to leave.

The profit that her 'owners' make from her is very large, as high as 800 per cent. Her annual turnover, the amount men pay for her, is more than $75,000—though she won't see a penny. These profits buy protection from the police, influence with local government, as well as social prestige. Her owners will be lucky to get five years' use from her since HIV is common in the brothels. But because she was so cheap, she is easily replaced. If she is ill or injured or just troublesome, she's disposable.

Slave-made goods

The brothels of Thailand are just one of the places where new slavery can be found. Slaves tend to be used in simple, non-technological and traditional work. Most work in agriculture. But they are also found in brick-making, mining and quarrying, textiles, leather-working, prostitution, gem-working and jewelry-making, cloth and carpet-making. Or they may work as domestic servants, clear forests, make charcoal or work in shops. Most of this work is aimed at local sale and consumption but slave-made goods filter through the entire global economy and may even end up in Western homes.

Studies have documented the slave origins of several international products such as carpets, sugar and jewellery. We may be using slave-made goods or investing in slavery without knowing it. Slave-produced cocoa, for example, goes into the chocolate we buy. Rugs made by slave children in India, Pakistan and Nepal are mainly exported to Europe and the US. The value of global slavery is estimated at $12.3 billion per year, including a significant amount of international trade in slave-produced goods. Despite this outrage few Northern businesses or organizations are taking action. Most trade associations argue that it is impossible to trace the twisted path to a product's origin or, more bluntly, that it's simply not their responsibility. The World Trade Organization has the power to introduce a 'social clause' to block products of forced labour, but it has not done so. And while 'fair trade' programmes are important alternatives to exploitation, they do not directly address the needs of enslaved workers. Obviously, there are many questions yet to be answered both about the economics of slavery and about the most effective strategies for abolition.

Recent studies show that human trafficking is increasing. The US Central Intelligence Agency estimates more than 50,000 persons a year are trafficked into the US. The UN Centre for International Crime Prevention says trafficking is now the third largest money earner for organized crime after drugs and guns. But a lack of reliable information means that governments are scrambling to build databases, develop effective interdiction, work out ways to free and rehabilitate trafficking victims, develop laws and conduct the research needed to address the issue.

Desperate for work and tricked by promises of a good job, [slaves] can be purchased in village markets for $40 per person.

Business is also pressed to deal with recent revelations of slavery amongst their suppliers. The filming of slaves on cocoa plantations in Côte d'Ivoire last year led to calls for a boycott of chocolate. Côte d'Ivoire produces about half of the world's cocoa. Some local activists claim that up to 90 per cent of the country's plantations use slave labour. Chocolate-producing companies have promised their own investigation.

The situation in Côte d'Ivoire encapsulates much of contemporary slavery. Slaves on the cocoa plantations are mostly from Mali. Desperate for work and tricked by promises of a good job, they can be purchased in village markets for $40 per person. The plantation owners who enslave them are facing a dramatic fall in the world price of cocoa as a result of the World Bank forcing an end to the state marketing monopoly. Meanwhile, Côte d'Ivoire carries $13.5 billion in debt to the Bank and other lenders. With debt payments five times greater than the nation's health-care budget, there are few resources to protect the enslaved migrants producing its key cash crop.

Exporting slaves

As well as importing, traffickers in West Africa export slaves to richer countries. Educated young women from Ghana and Cameroon, lured with a chance of further study in the US, have been enslaved as domestics in Washington DC. Large numbers of Nigerian women have been forced into prostitution in Italy. This human traffic into and out of the African coast is mirrored in many countries of the developing and developed world.

In Pakistan and India, across North Africa, in Southeast Asia and in Central and South America, more traditional forms of debt bondage enslave up to 20 million people. These slaves who may be in their third or fourth generation of bondage contribute little to export markets. Laws on bonded labour are either not strict enough, or not enforced. Police are often ignorant of those laws or, as in Brazil and Thailand, they may be profiting from bonded labour themselves.

The result is that underfunded non-governmental organizations bear the brunt of liberating slaves, sometimes in the face of government resistance. And liberation is just the first step in returning slaves to a life of freedom.

Think for a moment about the 43 children rescued from the Benin slave ship. Questions about their future are every bit as perplexing as questions about their recent past. Many child slaves have suffered physical and psychological abuse and require help. Nearly all have to adjust both to freedom and the challenge of earning a living. With luck, rehabilitation programmes will help them. But few governments are involved in this work.

If there is any good news about modern slavery, it is the dramatic growth in media interest and public awareness. The global coverage of the slave ship was just one example. The UN has several new initiatives on slavery and trafficking, as does the European Union. At the same time, anti-slavery organizations are experiencing an upturn in interest. As one representative of Anti-Slavery International explained recently: 'It is heartening, after years of neglect, to be part of a global movement against slavery. It is still in its infancy, but it is growing every day.'

6

World Leaders Must Combat Slavery Worldwide

Richard Re

Richard Re is a senior editor at the Harvard International Review, *a quarterly journal of international relations.*

Slavery today is an international problem. A decades-old civil war in Sudan has resulted in government-sanctioned kidnapping and enslavement of thousands of Sudanese. In addition, poor women and children from countries such as Thailand and Nigeria are lured into sex slavery by false offers of lucrative jobs in foreign countries. In order to combat the problem of slavery, world leaders must work to address its underlying causes—poverty, corrupt national governments, and unenforceable antislavery legislation.

Slavery has not been abolished. Although centuries of struggle and sacrifice on the part of anti-slavery activists have successfully made slavery illegal under international law, abolitionism triumph remains incomplete in reality. Conservative estimates indicate that at least 27 million people, in places as diverse as Nigeria, Indonesia, and Brazil, live in conditions of forced bondage. Some sources believe the actual figures are 10 times as large. To put these numbers in perspective, it is believed that 13 million slaves were taken from Africa through the trans-Atlantic slave trade that ended in the 19th century. Slavery statistics are so uncertain because surprisingly little data on the precise number, conditions, and locations of the world's slaves have been collected, a sign of the developed world's disregard for this rampant form of human-rights abuse. Such apathy is especially disturbing in light of the role the world's economic and political powers play in the continuation of this hideous practice, and could play in its termination.

Popular misconceptions about the end of slavery are in part due to the vast changes in the nature of slavery that have come about in the last 100 years. Whereas slavery was once a major financial institution that provided a foundation for many of the world's leading economies, organized mass slavery is now limited to the developing world, where a

Richard Re, "A Persisting Evil: The Global Problem of Slavery," *Harvard International Review*, vol. 23, Winter 2002, pp. 32–36. Copyright © 2002 by Harvard International Relations Council, Inc. Reproduced by permission.

tremendous population boom has made human beings a readily available commodity. In the antebellum United States, slaves were expensive and so were generally kept healthy and fit to work for as long as possible. Now, slaves are cheap. An Indian fabric manufacturer today can purchase a child slave for one five-thousandth of what it would have cost a Mississippi plantation owner to purchase a field worker in 1850, in adjusted and converted money. Slaves now are worked to death or discarded instantly by their masters when health conditions impede their work. To be discarded is often to live in abject poverty away from any family, crippled by physical and psychological injuries.

There have of course been other significant changes in the nature of slavery over the course of the last century. Before potential solutions and responses to the problem can be evaluated, it is necessary to illustrate some of these changes.

Slavery in Sudan

The relatively well-publicized and studied slave trade in Sudan represents a kind of slavery especially common in Africa. Sudanese slaves are captured during military raids performed and supported by their own government. Northern Sudan, which is primarily Arab and Muslim, militarily dominates the comparatively defenseless southerners, who tend to be black and Christian or of a more moderate version of Islam than supported by the ruling North. In the raids, conducted by militias called *murabaleen*, men are killed while women and children are captured and put to various kinds of work, sometimes laborious, sometimes sexual. Perhaps 90,000 Sudanese have been enslaved and brutalized in this manner.

The Sudanese government in Khartoum has denied that slavery exists within its borders, but human-rights advocates have demonstrated that the government actually arms slave raiders, who are compensated for their troubles with the right to steal from their victims. Khartoum might be using the slavers to depopulate parts of the southern country that agitate for independence or that stood in the way of the construction of a lucrative oil pipeline that is part of The Greater Nile Oil Project. This project was funded by foreign capital, especially from the Talisman Corporation, which operates in China, Malaysia, and Canada. Activists claim that this pipeline has fueled not industry; but a human-rights catastrophe.

> *Desperation and hope leave all too vulnerable those people most determined to escape inhumane conditions.*

Slaves taken in war, sometimes as part of an economy that sustains a war or civil conflict like the one in Sudan, are an increasingly common phenomenon. The tendency to enslave children on account of their particular helplessness is another lesson taken from Sudan's example. In other ways, Sudanese slavery is anomalous. It is based largely on racial and religious differences, following the model of Western slavery and imperialism. In contrast, the slave trade of the 21st century is largely indiscriminate when it comes to racial or ideological qualities of potential slaves. In fact, masters and slaves tend to be different only in that one possesses overwhelming physical power over the other.

Sex slavery

Another increasingly common tactic for 21st-century slavers is to lure the desperate and naive away from home and, unwittingly, into bondage. This is certainly a less inexpensive way of approaching slavery than the military operations that for millennia supplied the world's slave market. The world's vast disparities in wealth, education, and opportunity make this kind of slavery possible. Desperation and hope leave all too vulnerable those people most determined to escape inhumane conditions.

This tactic is usually used to target girls and young women. Impoverished families in rural areas recognize a greater economic value in their male children and are often motivated by patriarchal cultural mores. When well-dressed men come offering a small monetary down payment (in one documented case, less than US$25) to transport girls away from home to work as maids or waitresses or in other plausible occupations, these families often jump at the opportunity. In reality, these men are slavers who take their willing cargo to the city to be "broken in" for their life of involuntary prostitution. The girls are sometimes beaten, raped, starved, or tortured until they submit to their keepers' demands. From this point in their lives, the girls have few options open to them as they are traded and sold into new regions and nations. Gates and chains keep them from leaving, but so do threats, isolation, poverty, and the fear of stigmatization if they return to their homes. Their careers usually end when they contract AIDS and are either deposited in a slum or allowed to die when they cease to earn profit for their owners. Few escape this fate.

Slavery is necessarily involved in some kind of economic activity.

In Mumbai, some 90,000 sex slaves work in the city's red light district. Virgins and children are preferred by wealthier clients because they have less likelihood of being HIV positive. Some 20,000 Burmese girls are believed to be held in Thai brothels. Sex slaves have been lured into lives of prostitution and exported to Western Europe, where hundreds of Nigerian girls were told they would find better lives. Enticed by the promise, they accepted, and were shipped to brothels in the Netherlands, Italy, Germany, Greece, and elsewhere. In the last few years, brothels in California and New York were independently discovered to have bought Thai slaves for about US$10,000 and held them trapped in sealed buildings. Shackles, barbed wire, and the danger of falling dozens of feet from one building's upper floors kept the women from escaping.

Sometimes sex slaves like these women are not considered slaves but indentured laborers because the girls are made to work off their "debt" incurred by transportation and housing costs. But this is merely what the girls and their families are told. The psychological effects of establishing rules and procedures for leaving the brothel and implying that it was the girls' own choice (and fault) that they are in their predicament are advantageous to the slaver who is indeed applying the threat of physical force to compel involuntary but highly profitable labor. This is slavery concealed, but slavery nonetheless.

Redemption

The international responses to Sudan's situation, probably the best publicized of any slave trade in the world, represent virtually every major perspective on the issue. Some humanitarians, frustrated with governments' inability to address the problem in any direct way, have made trips to Africa to buy slaves and free them from bondage. This process of redemption is perhaps best exemplified by two initiatives.

One began in 1998 when Barbara Vogel, a fifth-grade teacher, read an article about Sudanese slavery to her class. When the children responded with a desire to help, she organized their sympathies into the STOP (Slavery That Oppresses People) Campaign, a nationwide movement that raised awareness in elementary and grade schools with the aim of gathering funds to redeem slaves in the Sudan. In two years, STOP's efforts impressed Colorado Representative Tom Tancredo enough for him to declare, "This fifth grade class from Colorado has done more for the people of Sudan than the entire United States government."

The second example, the story of Harvard University student Jay Williams, follows similar lines. As a freshman, Williams heard about global slavery from a speaker at a gospel music concert. He immediately began to address the issue through an internship with the American Anti-Slavery Group (AASG). His efforts culminated in a trip to Sudan before his sophomore year in which Williams and the AASG purchased the freedom of over 4,400 slaves. In the summer of 2001, Williams did it again, traveling to Sudan with members of the AASG and liberating almost 7,000 slaves in a week and a half. Many of these slaves had been physically brutalized; about 80 percent of the women reported sexual abuse. John Eibner, a Christian Solidarity leader who himself helped redeem thousands of slaves, summarizes the attitude of these and other redemption efforts when he proclaims, "We can all combat evil."

Yet US government officials and the UN Children's Fund (UNICEF) have warned against redemption as a means to combat slavery. According to them, to purchase slaves, even to free them, is still to contribute to the profitability of the slave trade by raising the demand for slaves. Redemption therefore helps sustain the slave market and encourages the enslavement of more innocent people. Further, massive redemption operations like the ones described above would probably have a significant impact on the price of slaves, making it harder or impossible for relatively poor Sudanese to afford to free their own people. Redemption advocates sometimes claim that the market price for slaves has not changed as a result of their operations and that, if the price did increase, they would be willing to cease their operations. Usually, though, people involved in the redemption movement respond to criticism by invoking the ineffable and constant suffering of slaves as grounds for a moral imperative to address the problem. Cooler heads, and economists, are not so easily persuaded.

Redemption efforts are frequently compared with the operations of the Underground Railroad that combated slavery in the United States. This comparison is faulty in important and revealing ways. Abolitionists in the United States came to support radical action to permanently end slavery in their nation. They were willing to risk war to eradicate slavery through legal, not financial, measures. The Underground Railroad did not buy slaves. It helped them escape. It resisted involvement in the sale of humanity.

These direct measures are not available to antislavery organizations in the United States today. There is not enough popular outrage to justify a major war of liberation half the world away, and there is no international law with any coercive power to hear their appeals. Faced with the choice between funding redemption campaigns and watching their governments apply international economic and political pressure on the slave-fostering nations, a process that might take decades to bear fruit, it is easy to understand why humanitarians are drawn to the faster, and in many ways surer, form of aid.

Solving the problem

Of course, redemption efforts, whether carried out in Sudanese auctions or in Thai brothels, in Pakistani textile factories or in Brazilian coal mines, can never hope to address slavery's underlying causes. These include poverty in the developing world, the corruption and inhumanity of national governments, and the lack of enforceable global legislation when it comes to the protection of basic human rights. Concerted international efforts by government agencies are required. To the extent that anti-slavery activists draw attention to the existence of global slavery, their work makes it more likely that nations will work to end this hideous practice. But they must make it clear to the public that writing checks and making brief tours through slave lands constitute a treatment at best, and not a solution.

Unlike other massive human-rights violations that take place in the contemporary world, slavery is necessarily involved in some kind of economic activity. In an ever more globalized world, economic productivity becomes entangled in financial systems that stretch beyond the borders of any one nation. Whether it is through foreign direct investment (FDI), which has been cited as providing the economic incentive for the slave raids of Sudan, or international trade, like the sale of Thai prostitutes to US and European brothels, slave labor involves people from all regions of the world. Neither the causes nor the effects of slave labor are limited to the slaves and masters themselves.

In one way, this view makes the existence of mass slavery even more morally troubling, since it becomes impossible for nations geographically distant from the main site of slave activity to completely absolve themselves of responsibility. But it is also encouraging because it means that slavery, unlike potentially localized atrocities like genocide and famine, is vulnerable to ethical decisions made by people who can become aware of their indirect involvement in the slave trade. As a company executive or political leader or even as a common consumer, members of the developed world can make market choices that make slavery unprofitable.

Some steps in this direction have already been taken. It is now illegal for a US citizen to cross borders to have sex with a slave. In 2001, the [George W.] Bush administration took steps to increase executive control over foreign direct investment (FDI) that might contribute to slave conditions. And, on his most recent trip to Sudan, Jay Williams researched the connection between FDI and slave conditions in the region, returning with exhortations for investors to put pressure on companies whose activities indirectly encourage enslavement. These beginnings are humble and certainly far less dramatic than raids on slave colonies or magnanimous efforts to buy back the world's slaves. But there is considerable hope that, with time and resolve, measures like these might address the root causes of human bondage and leave slavery, at last, truly abolished.

7

The United States Must Work to Abolish Slavery

Christopher H. Smith

Christopher H. Smith, a Republican representative from New Jersey, is vice chairman of the House Committee on International Relations.

Human trafficking is a global atrocity that victimizes millions of people each year. To combat the problem of human trafficking and slavery, the United States passed the Trafficking Victims Protection Act of 2000. Among other provisions, the act requires the state department to rank countries according to their efforts to reduce slavery and trafficking in humans. Although the act is a useful tool in the fight against slavery, more must be done to prevent future occurrences of such gross human rights violations. The United States must lead the way toward a world free of human trafficking and slavery.

The United States abolished legalized slavery nearly 140 years ago, but today a new scourge of human slavery remains and thrives throughout the world. Americans need to know the reality of human trafficking and our government needs to exert its fullest strength to end this appalling human rights abuse.

An estimated 700,000 to 4 million victims of human trafficking are bought, sold, transported and held against their will in slave-like conditions each year. Most victims are women and children.

Many are lured from their homes with promises of a better life by cunning traffickers who force them to work in brothels as sex slaves or as forced laborers in sweatshops, as domestic servants, or beggars, to name just a few scenarios. Violence is commonly used to control victims and maintain their servitude. In cases of forced prostitution, victims are repeatedly raped every day and are forced to cope in subhuman conditions.

Recently, the State Department released its second annual "Trafficking in Persons" (TIP) report, which evaluates the efforts of 89 countries in combating the modern-day slavery of human trafficking. The TIP report is a tool created by the Trafficking Victims Protection Act, a law that I

Christopher H. Smith, "Modern Slavery," *The Washington Times*, June 18, 2002, p. A19.

sponsored to assess the progress made in combating the scourge of trafficking in human beings around the world. The law requires the State Department to rank countries' efforts to meet minimum standards to combat trafficking and whether those countries are making "significant efforts" to bring itself into compliance with those standards.

It is imperative that the United States and foreign governments exert more effort to eliminate the scourge of human slavery.

When the law was enacted in 2000, many in Congress and the administration did not want to publicly name offending countries. Other policymakers, myself included, argued that some countries only get serious about addressing their failures to combat slavery if their deficiencies are publicly identified. My two year's experience with the TIP report supports that argument: During the year between the first and the second reports, the governments of more than two dozen countries improved their behavior and policies enough to merit an improved mark. Only two countries—Cambodia and the Kyrgyz Republic—dropped in ranking from the first year to the second.

It is clear the Bush administration devoted substantial time, effort and personnel to prepare the 2002 TIP report. The report will continue to serve as a useful tool for diplomats and members of Congress as we engage our foreign counterparts regarding their efforts to combat human trafficking.

Nonetheless, the TIP report is not flawless. India, Thailand and Vietnam, among others, received better rankings than they deserved despite credible reports indicating their efforts to combat trafficking were clearly insignificant in light of the enormity of the human trafficking problems in those countries. More than 2.3 million girls and women are believed to be working in the sex industry against their will at any given time—possibly as many as 40 percent are children. In India, for example, more than 200,000 persons are trafficked in the country each year. Indian boys, some as young as age 4, are trafficked abroad to be enslaved and brutalized as camel jockeys in camel races. Evidence exists that law-enforcement and government officials help facilitate human trafficking, that investigations and prosecutions of traffickers are rare, and that local corruption renders most prosecutorial efforts ineffective. Nonetheless, the State Department deemed India to be making "significant efforts" to combat trafficking.

As we move forward, it is imperative that the United States and foreign governments exert more effort to eliminate the scourge of human slavery. The United States must be resolute in ensuring that governments that do not seriously combat trafficking will receive and retain the lowest possible ranking until they mend their ways. We must also ensure that even our allies are not given a free pass if the facts show they are not doing enough to address modern-day slavery. If the report is to continue to be an effective document, it must honestly evaluate countries according to the evidence.

Above all, the United States must lead by example. Despite the U.S.

government's many initiatives to prevent and punish trafficking in human beings here and abroad, I recently received disturbing information that some U.S. military personnel stationed in South Korea are patrons of brothels where trafficked women are enslaved in forced prostitution. U.S. military personnel appear to have knowledge that these women are forced to prostitute themselves and, perhaps most disturbingly, their actions appear to be taking place with the knowledge and tacit consent of their commanding officers.

The Pentagon must act expeditiously to clean up its act in this regard. I and other members of the House and Senate have requested Defense Secretary Donald Rumsfeld to launch an immediate and thorough investigation into U.S. soldiers' unconscionable exploitation of enslaved women, while fighting to defend freedom and liberty abroad.

While we are making progress in our fight against human trafficking, the sheer number of victims worldwide—possibly as many as half the population of my home state of New Jersey—underscores the gravity of this problem and the vast amount of work still to be done.

8

Sex Slavery Must
Be Eradicated

Alice Leuchtag

*Freelance writer Alice Leuchtag has worked as a social worker, coun-
selor, college instructor, and researcher. Active in the civil rights, peace,
socialist, feminist, and humanist movements, she has helped organize
women in Houston, Texas, to oppose sex trafficking.*

Poor women and children throughout the world are deceived into
accepting job offers that turn out to be forced sex work. Victims
are made to have sex with hundreds of men to repay pimps for
their transportation costs, housing, food, and medical care. Under
pressure from human rights organizations, world leaders have
drafted international legislation that will punish people who traffic in humans and protect trafficked prostitutes. Human rights
groups also propose increasing punishments for people who are
caught buying sex from enslaved sex workers. Although some nations have sought to address the problems associated with prostitution by legalizing it, legalization is not the answer; ending sexual exploitation is the only way to stop the distortion of human
sexuality and build true respect between men and women.

Despite laws against slavery in practically every country, an estimated
twenty-seven million people live as slaves. Kevin Bales, in his book
Disposable People: New Slavery in the Global Economy (University of California Press, Berkeley, 1999), describes those who endure modern forms
of slavery. These include indentured servants, persons held in hereditary
bondage, child slaves who pick plantation crops, child soldiers, and
adults and children trafficked and sold into sex slavery.

A life narrative

Of all forms of slavery, sex slavery is one of the most exploitative and lucrative with some 200,000 sex slaves worldwide bringing their slaveholders an annual profit of $10.5 billion. Although the great preponderance
of sex slaves are women and girls, a smaller but significant number of

Alice Leuchtag, "Human Rights, Sex Trafficking, and Prostitution," *The Humanist*, vol. 63, January/
February 2003, pp. 10–16. Copyright © 2003 by the American Humanist Association. Reproduced
by permission.

males—both adult and children—are enslaved for homosexual prostitution. The life narrative of a Thai girl named Siri, as told to Bales, illustrates how sex slavery happens to vulnerable girls and women. Siri is born in northeastern Thailand to a poor family that farms a small plot of land, barely eking out a living. Economic policies of structural adjustment pursued by the Thai government under the aegis of the World Bank and the International Monetary Fund have taken former government subsidies away from rice farmers, leaving them to compete against imported, subsidized rice that keeps the market price artificially depressed.

Siri attends four years of school, then is kept at home to help care for her three younger siblings. When Siri is fourteen, a well-dressed woman visits her village. She offers to find Siri a "good job," advancing her parents $2,000 against future earnings. This represents at least a year's income for the family. In a town in another province the woman, a trafficker, "sells" Siri to a brothel for $4,000. Owned by an "investment club" whose members are business and professional men—government bureaucrats and local politicians—the brothel is extremely profitable. In a typical thirty-day period it nets its investors $88,000.

To maintain the appearance that their hands are clean, members of the club's board of directors leave the management of the brothel to a pimp and a bookkeeper. Siri is initiated into prostitution by the pimp who rapes her. After being abused by her first "customer," Siri escapes, but a policeman—who gets a percentage of the brothel profits—brings her back, whereupon the pimp beats her up. As further punishment, her "debt" is doubled from $4,000 to $8,000. She must now repay this, along with her monthly rent and food, all from her earnings of $4 per customer. She will have to have sex with three hundred men a month just to pay her rent. Realizing she will never be able to get out of debt, Siri tries to build a relationship with the pimp simply in order to survive.

Sex tourism creates a business climate conducive to the trafficking and enslavement of vulnerable girls.

The pimp uses culture and religion to reinforce his control over Siri. He tells her she must have committed terrible sins in a past life to have been born a female; she must have accumulated a karmic debt to deserve the enslavement and abuse to which she must reconcile herself. Gradually Siri begins to see herself from the point of view of the slaveholder—as someone unworthy and deserving of punishment. By age fifteen she no longer protests or runs away. Her physical enslavement has become psychological as well, a common occurrence in chronic abuse.

Siri is administered regular injections of the contraceptive drug Depo-Provera for which she is charged. As the same needle is used for all the girls, there is a high risk of HIV and other sexual diseases from the injections. Siri knows that a serious illness threatens her and she prays to Buddha at the little shrine in her room, hoping to earn merit so he will protect her from dreaded disease. Once a month she and the others, at their own expense, are tested for HIV. So far Siri's tests have been negative. When Siri tries to get the male customers to wear condoms—distributed free to brothels by the Thai Ministry of Health—some resist wearing them and she can't make them do so.

As one of an estimated 35,000 women working as brothel slaves in Thailand—a country where 500,000 to one million prostituted women and girls work in conditions of degradation and exploitation short of brothel slavery—Siri faces at least a 40 percent chance of contracting the HIV virus. If she is lucky, she can look forward to five more years before she becomes too ill to work and is pushed out into the street.

Thailand's sex tourism

Though the Thai government denies it, the Health Organization finds that HIV is epidemic in Thailand, with the largest segment of new cases among wives and girlfriends of men who buy prostitute sex. Viewing its women as a cash crop to be exploited, and depending on sex tourism for foreign exchange dollars to help pay interest on the foreign debt, the Thai government can't acknowledge the epidemic without contradicting the continued promotion of sex tourism and prostitution.

By encouraging investment in the sex industry, sex tourism creates a business climate conducive to the trafficking and enslavement of vulnerable girls such as Siri. In 1996 nearly five million sex tourists from the United States, Western Europe, Australia, and Japan visited Thailand. These transactions brought in about $26.2 billion—thirteen times more than Thailand earned by building and exporting computers.

In her 1999 report *Pimps and Predators on the Internet: Globalizing the Sexual Exploitation of Women and Children*, published by the Coalition Against Trafficking in Women (CATW), Donna Hughes quotes from postings on an Internet site where sex tourists share experiences and advise one another. The following is one man's description of having sex with a fourteen-year-old prostituted girl in Bangkok:

> Even though I've had a lot of better massages . . . after fifteen minutes, I was much more relaxed. . . . Then I asked for a condom and I fucked her for another thirty minutes. Her face looked like she was feeling a lot of pain. . . . She blocked my way when I wanted to leave the room and she asked for a tip. I gave her 600 baht. Altogether, not a good experience.

Hughes says, "To the men who buy sex, a 'bad experience' evidently means not getting their money's worth, or that the prostituted woman or girl didn't keep up the act of enjoying what she had to do . . . one glimpses the humiliation and physical pain most girls and women in prostitution endure."

Nor are the men oblivious to the existence of sexual slavery. One customer states, "Girls in Bangkok virtually get sold by their families into the industry; they work against their will." His knowledge of their sexual slavery and lack of sensitivity thereof is evident in that he then names the hotels in which girls are kept and describes how much they cost!

As Hughes observes, sex tourists apparently feel they have a right to prostitute sex, perceiving prostitution only from a self-interested perspective in which they commodify and objectify women of other cultures, nationalities, and ethnic groups. Their awareness of racism, colonialism, global economic inequalities, and sexism seems limited to the way these realities benefit them as sex consumers.

Sex traffickers cast their nets

According to the Guide to the New UN Trafficking Protocol by Janice Raymond, published by the CATW in 2001, the United Nations estimates that sex trafficking in human beings is a $5 billion to $7 billion operation annually. Four million persons are moved illegally from one country to another and within countries each year, a large proportion of them women and girls being trafficked into prostitution. The United Nations International Children's Emergency Fund (UNICEF) estimates that some 30 percent of women being trafficked are minors, many under age thirteen. The International Organization on Migration estimates that some 500,000 women per year are trafficked into Western Europe from poorer regions of the world. According to *Sex Trafficking of Women in the United States: International and Domestic Trends*, also published by the CATW in 2001, some 50,000 women and children are trafficked into the United States each year, mainly from Asia and Latin America.

Because prostitution as a system of organized sexual exploitation depends on a continuous supply of new "recruits," trafficking is essential to its continued existence. When the pool of available women and girls dries up, new women must be procured. Traffickers cast their nets ever wider and become ever more sophisticated. The Italian Camorra, Chinese Triads, Russian Mafia, and Japanese Yakuza are powerful criminal syndicates consisting of traffickers, pimps, brothel keepers, forced labor lords, and gangs which operate globally.

After the breakdown of the Soviet Union, an estimated five thousand criminal groups formed the Russian Mafia, which operates in thirty countries. The Russian Mafia traffics women from African countries, the Ukraine, the Russian Federation, and Eastern Europe into Western Europe, the United States, and Israel. The Triads traffick women from China, Korea, Thailand, and other Southeast Asian countries into the United States and Europe. The Camorra traffics women from Latin America into Europe. The Yakuza traffics women from the Philippines, Thailand, Burma, Cambodia, Korea, Nepal, and Laos into Japan.

A global problem meets a global response

Despite these appalling facts, until recently no generally agreed upon definition of trafficking in human beings was written into international law. In Vienna, Austria, during 1999 and 2000, 120 countries participated in debates over a definition of trafficking. A few nongovernmental organizations (NGOs) and a minority of governments—including Australia, Canada, Denmark, Germany, Ireland, Japan, the Netherlands, Spain, Switzerland, Thailand, and the United Kingdom—wanted to separate issues of trafficking from issues of prostitution. They argued that persons being trafficked should be divided into those who are forced and those who give their consent, with the burden of proof being placed on persons being trafficked. They also urged that the less explicit means of control over trafficked persons—such as abuse of a victim's vulnerability—not be included in the definition of trafficking and that the word exploitation not be used. Generally supporters of this position were wealthier countries where large numbers of women were being trafficked and countries in which prostitution was legalized or sex tourism encouraged.

The CATW—140 other NGOs that make up the International Human Rights Network plus many governments (including those of Algeria, Bangladesh, Belgium, China, Colombia, Cuba, Egypt, Finland, France, India, Mexico, Norway, Pakistan, the Philippines, Sweden, Syria, Venezuela, and Vietnam)—maintains that trafficking can't be separated from prostitution. Persons being trafficked shouldn't be divided into those who are forced and those who give their consent because trafficked persons are in no position to give meaningful consent. The subtler methods used by traffickers, such as abuse of a victim's vulnerability, should be included in the definition of trafficking and the word exploitation be an essential part of the definition. Generally supporters of this majority view were poorer countries from which large numbers of women were being trafficked or countries in which strong feminist, anti-colonialist, or socialist influences existed. The United States, though initially critical of the majority position, agreed to support a definition of trafficking that would be agreed upon by consensus.

Because prostitution as a system of organized sexual exploitation depends on a continuous supply of new "recruits," trafficking is essential to its continued existence.

The struggle—led by the CATW to create a definition of trafficking that would penalize traffickers while ensuring that all victims of trafficking would be protected—succeeded when a compromise proposal by Sweden was agreed to. A strongly worded and inclusive UN Protocol to Prevent, Suppress, and Punish Trafficking in Persons—especially women and children—was drafted by an ad hoc committee of the UN as a supplement to the Convention Against Transnational Organized Crime. The UN protocol specifically addresses the trade in human beings for purposes of prostitution and other forms of sexual exploitation, forced labor or services, slavery or practices similar to slavery, servitude, and the removal of organs. The protocol defines trafficking as:

> The recruitment, transportation, transfer, harboring or receipt of persons, by means of the threat or use of force or other forms of coercion, of abduction, of fraud, of deception, of the abuse of power or of a position of vulnerability or of the giving or receiving of payments or benefits to achieve the consent of a person having control over another person, for the purpose of exploitation.

While recognizing that the largest amount of trafficking involves women and children, the wording of the UN protocol clearly is gender and age neutral, inclusive of trafficking in both males and females, adults and children.

In 2000 the UN General Assembly adopted this convention and its supplementary protocol; 121 countries signed the convention and eighty countries signed the protocol. For the convention and protocol to become international law, forty countries must ratify them.

Highlights

Some highlights of the new convention and protocol are:

For the first time there is an accepted international definition of trafficking and an agreed-upon set of prosecution, protection, and prevention mechanisms on which countries can base their national legislation.

• The various criminal means by which trafficking takes place, including indirect and subtle forms of coercion, are covered.

• Trafficked persons, especially women in prostitution and child laborers, are no longer viewed as illegal migrants but as victims of a crime.

• The convention doesn't limit its scope to criminal syndicates but defines an organized criminal group as "any structured group of three or more persons which engages in criminal activities such as trafficking and pimping."

• All victims of trafficking in persons are protected, not just those who can prove that force was used against them.

• The consent of a victim of trafficking is meaningless and irrelevant.

• Victims of trafficking won't have to bear the burden of proof.

• Trafficking and sexual exploitation are intrinsically connected and not to be separated.

• Because women trafficked domestically into local sex industries suffer harmful effects similar to those experienced by women trafficked transnationally, these women also come under the protections of the protocol.

• The key element in trafficking is the exploitative purpose rather than the movement across a border.

The protocol is the first UN instrument to address the demand for prostitution sex, a demand that results in the human rights abuses of women and children being trafficked. The protocol recognizes an urgent need for governments to put the buyers of prostitution sex on their policy and legislative agendas, and it calls upon countries to take or strengthen legislative or other measures to discourage demand, which fosters all the forms of sexual exploitation of women and children.

As Raymond says in the *Guide to the New UN Trafficking Protocol:*

> The least discussed part of the prostitution and trafficking chain has been the men who buy women for sexual exploitation in prostitution. . . . If we are to find a permanent path to ending these human rights abuses, then we cannot just shrug our shoulders and say, "men are like this," or "boys will be boys," or "prostitution has always been around." Or tell women and girls in prostitution that they must continue to do what they do because prostitution is inevitable. Rather, our responsibility is to make men change their behavior, by all means available—educational, cultural and legal.

Two U.S. feminist human rights organizations—Captive Daughters and Equality Now—have been working toward that goal. Surita Sandosham of Equality Now says that when her organization asked women's groups in Thailand and the Philippines how it could assist them, the answer came back, "Do something about the demand." Since then the two organizations have legally challenged sex tours originating in the United States and have succeeded in closing down at least one operation.

Refugees, not illegal aliens

In October 2000 the U.S. Congress passed a bill, the Victims of Trafficking and Violence Protection Act of 2000, introduced by New Jersey republican representative Chris Smith. Under this law penalties for traffickers are raised and protections for victims increased. Reasoning that desperate women are unable to give meaningful consent to their own sexual exploitation, the law adopts a broad definition of sex trafficking so as not to exclude so-called consensual prostitution or trafficking that occurs solely within the United States. In these respects the new federal law conforms to the UN protocol.

Two features of the law are particularly noteworthy:

• In order to pressure other countries to end sex trafficking, the U.S. State Department is to make a yearly assessment of other countries' anti-trafficking efforts and to rank them according to how well they discourage trafficking. After two years of failing to meet even minimal standards, countries are subject to sanctions, although not sanctions on humanitarian aid. "Tier 3" countries—those failing to meet even minimal standards—include Greece, Indonesia, Israel, Pakistan, Russia, Saudi Arabia, South Korea, and Thailand.

• Among persons being trafficked into the United States, special T-visas will be provided to those who meet the criteria for having suffered the most serious trafficking abuses. These visas will protect them from deportation so they can testify against their traffickers. T-non immigrant status allows eligible aliens to remain in the United States temporarily and grants specific non-immigrant benefits. Those acquiring T-1 non-immigrant status will be able to remain for a period of three years and will be eligible to receive certain kinds of public assistance—to the same extent as refugees. They will also be issued employment authorization to "assist them in finding safe, legal employment while they attempt to retake control of their lives."

A debate rages

A worldwide debate rages about legalization of prostitution fueled by a 1998 International Labor Organization (ILO) report entitled *The Sex Sector: The Economic and Social Bases of Prostitution in Southeast Asia*. The report follows years of lobbying by the sex industry for recognition of prostitution as "sex work." Citing the sex industry's unrecognized contribution to the gross domestic product of four countries in Southeast Asia, the ILO urges governments to officially recognize the "sex sector" and "extend taxation nets to cover many of the lucrative activities connected with it." Though the ILO report says it stops short of calling for legalization of prostitution, official recognition of the sex industry would be impossible without it.

Raymond points out that the ILO's push to redefine prostitution as sex work ignores legislation demonstrating that countries can reduce organized sexual exploitation rather than capitulate to it. For example, Sweden prohibits the purchase of sexual services with punishments of stiff fines or imprisonment, thus declaring that prostitution isn't a desirable economic and labor sector. The government also helps women getting out of prostitution to rebuild their lives. Venezuela's Ministry of Labor has ruled that prostitution can't be considered work because it lacks the basic elements of dignity and social justice. The Socialist Republic of Vietnam punishes pimps, traffickers, brothel owners, and buyers—sometimes publishing buyer's names in the mass media. For women in prostitution, the government finances medical, educational, and economic rehabilitation.

Raymond suggests that instead of transforming the male buyer into a legitimate customer, the ILO should give thought to innovative programs that make the buyer accountable for his sexual exploitation. She cites the Sage Project, Inc. (SAGE) program in San Francisco, California, which educates men arrested for soliciting women in prostitution about the risks and impacts of their behavior.

Legalization advocates argue that the violence, exploitation, and health effects suffered by women in prostitution aren't inherent to prostitution but simply result from the random behaviors of bad pimps or buyers, and that if prostitution were regulated by the state these harms would diminish. But examples show these arguments to be false.

In the pamphlet entitled *Legalizing Prostitution Is Not the Answer: The Example of Victoria, Australia*, published by the CATW in 2001, Mary Sullivan and Sheila Jeffreys describe the way legalization in Australia has perpetuated and strengthened the culture of violence and exploitation inherent in prostitution. Under legalization, legal and illegal brothels have proliferated, and trafficking in women has accelerated to meet the increased demand. Pimps, having even more power, continue threatening and brutalizing the women they control. Buyers continue to abuse women, refuse to wear condoms, and spread the HIV virus—and other sexually transmitted diseases—to their wives and girlfriends. Stigmatized by identity cards and medical inspections, prostituted women are even more marginalized and tightly locked into the system of organized sexual exploitation while the state, now an official party to the exploitation, has become the biggest pimp of all.

The government of the Netherlands has legalized prostitution, doesn't enforce laws against pimping, and virtually lives off taxes from the earnings of prostituted women. In the book *Making the Harm Visible* (published by the CATW in 1999), Marie-Victoire Louis describes the effects on prostituted women of municipal regulation of brothels in Amsterdam and other Dutch cities. Her article entitled "Legalizing Pimping, Dutch Style" explains the way immigration policies in the Netherlands are shaped to fit the needs of the prostitution industry so that traffickers are seldom prosecuted and a continuous supply of women is guaranteed. In Amsterdam's 250 officially listed brothels, 80 percent of the prostitutes have been trafficked in from other countries and 70 percent possess no legal papers. Without money, papers, or contact with the outside world, these immigrant women live in terror. Instead of being protected by the regulations governing brothels, prostituted women are frequently beaten up and raped by pimps. These "prostitution managers" have practically been given a free hand by the state and by buyers who, as "consumers of prostitution," feel themselves entitled to abuse the women they buy. Sadly and ironically the "Amsterdam model" of legalization and regulation is touted by the Netherlands and Germany as "self-determination and empowerment for women." In reality it simply legitimizes the "right" to buy, sexually use, and profit from the sexual exploitation of someone else's body.

A human rights approach

As part of a system of organized sexual exploitation, prostitution can be visualized along a continuum of abuse with brothel slavery at the furthest extreme. All along the continuum, fine lines divide the degrees of harm done to those caught up in the system. At the core lies a great social injustice no cosmetic reforms can right: the setting aside of a segment of people whose bodies can be purchased for sexual use by others. When this basic injustice is legitimized and regulated by the state and when the state profits from it, that injustice is compounded.

In her book *The Prostitution of Sexuality* (New York University Press, 1995), Kathleen Barry details a feminist human rights approach to prostitution that points the way to the future. Ethically it recognizes prostitution, sex trafficking, and the globalized industrialization of sex as massive violations of women's human rights. Sociologically it considers how and to what extent prostitution promotes sex discrimination against individual women, against different racial categories of women, and against women as a group. Politically it calls for decriminalizing prostitutes while penalizing pimps, traffickers, brothel owners, and buyers.

Understanding that human rights and restorative justice go hand in hand, the feminist human rights approach to prostitution addresses the harm and the need to repair the damage. As Barry says:

> Legal proposals to criminalize customers, based on the recognition that prostitution violates and harms women, must . . . include social-service, health and counseling and job retraining programs. Where states would be closing down brothels if customers were criminalized, the economic resources poured into the former prostitution areas could be turned toward producing gainful employment for women.

With the help of women's projects in many countries—such as Buklod in the Philippines and the Council for Prostitution Alternatives in the United States—some women have begun to confront their condition by leaving prostitution, speaking out against it, revealing their experiences, and helping other women leave the sex industry.

Ending the sexual exploitation of trafficking and prostitution will mean the beginning of a new chapter in building a humanist future—a more peaceful and just future in which men and women can join together in love and respect, recognizing one another's essential dignity and humanity. Humanity's sexuality then will no longer be hijacked and distorted.

9

Slave Redemption Has a Role in Combating Slavery in Sudan

Martin Arrowsmith

Martin Arrowsmith is a writer and activist based in Washington, D.C.

Many human rights organizations, particularly Christian Solidarity International, strive to liberate enslaved Sudanese by purchasing the slaves' freedom, a process known as redemption. Opponents of slave redemption argue that the practice actually perpetuates slavery by driving up the market price of slaves, making slave trading more profitable. However, in many communities, ineffective antislavery legislation and corrupt law enforcement provide substantial bulwarks to freeing slaves. In these countries, redemption is the only way to help victims escape slavery. Until local law enforcement in these communities enforces international laws against slavery, slave redemption may be the only way to liberate slaves.

In southern Sudan a western charity pays $50 per person to free Dinka people. They were enslaved after their villages were raided by militia linked to the Sudanese government. In northern India, a group of women band together to form a small credit union; over a period of months they save enough to repay the debt that holds one of their members in bondage, then they begin to save to buy another woman's freedom. In south India a child is freed from slavery when a charity pays off the man who has enslaved him to make beedi cigarettes. Today, with 27 million slaves in the world, redemption (making a payment to free a slave) can and does happen anywhere. But why is this happening? How can we understand the role of redemption in the global anti-slavery movement?

The history of slave redemption

While slave redemption has been in the news lately, it actually has a very long history. Slaves were being redeemed long before there was slavery in the U.S. In Greece, Rome, and other ancient societies, slaves were sometimes purchased from their owners and freed. During the Crusades, enslavement and ransom were central components of war finances and strategy. The first organizations that can be thought of as charities were set up in the Middle Ages in order to purchase the freedom of Europeans captured and enslaved by North African and Middle Eastern pirates and slave raiders. Indeed, the verse in the U.S. "Marine's Hymn"—to the shores of Tripoli—refers to an early 19th century raid on these Barbary pirates to stop their raiding, enslavement and ransoming of Europeans and Americans. Frederick Douglass, the famous 19th century abolitionist and escaped slave, was himself redeemed after supporters of slavery mounted a series of attempts at kidnapping him. The redeeming or ransoming of slaves probably goes back to the very beginnings of human slavery, to the very beginnings of written human history.

Before slavery was illegal in most countries, redemption was an act of charity, and itself perfectly legal. Many cultures have a tradition of redemption, including North African societies such as Sudan. Today, however, within the context of the general illegality of slavery, the buying of slaves, even to free them, is seen by many people as complicity in a crime.

Before slavery was illegal in most countries, redemption was an act of charity.

While redemption can go on around the world wherever slavery exists, it came to the attention of most Americans when groups like Christian Solidarity International began to buy back slaves in Sudan in 1995. Slave raiding in Sudan was part of the government's strategy to destroy the resistance of the southern groups fighting for independence. Slavery existed for hundreds of years in Sudan, almost disappeared in the 20th century, but was reestablished as an act of terror in the civil war there. Some international agencies expressed the criticism that buying back slaves would create an expanding market for slaves, feed resources to the slaveholders, lead to fraud in the process, and would not ultimately end slavery.

Not long after these criticisms emerged I spoke with a man from southern Sudan who answered in this way: "Of course we understand that the money paid to buy back our relatives may go to buy arms to be used against us in the future, but when it is your family, your children at stake, you pay." Likewise, a man involved in redemption pointed out that there may have been fraud (the "buying back" of people who had never been enslaved), but he asserted that "it is better to buy back some people who have never been slaves, than to fail to rescue the many who are suffering in slavery." On the question of whether redemption in Sudan has brought a greater risk of slave raids, there is insufficient evidence to make a clear judgment.

Consider the culture

The process of redemption must also be seen in its cultural context. The civil war has been marked by recurrent truces between the Dinka and the

Baggara tribesmen who make up the majority of the militia, truces that have provided the opportunity to recover, usually at a price, family members as well as livestock. Equally, the Nuer and Dinka tribes of southern Sudan, while now allied against the Muslim north, have long been in conflict that includes raiding between the two tribes. In early October 1999 their leaders met to discuss "the return of women, children, and cattle captured in raids or abducted during the years of hostility between the tribes." The fact that the victims of slave raiding have themselves raided other tribes has been rarely mentioned in the Western press.

[Slave redemption] is the lesser of several evils.

If there is good news about the controversy over redemption in Sudan it is that the civil war there has entered a new stage and fewer raids are taking place while peace talks continue. The U.S. government has become involved and has exerted significant pressure on the northern government to end the raids and come to an agreement with the southern provisional government. However, the hoped-for ending of the need for redemption in Sudan will not resolve the questions that surround redemption. On the other hand, this change may allow us to enlarge the discussion to include how redemption fits into anti-slavery work around the world.

In India, for example, redemption is actually illegal. In that country the primary form of slavery is "debt bondage" and the law that frees those in bondage forbids that their "debts" are repaid to bring about their freedom. The reason is that since these debts were offered and manipulated illegally in the first place, they have no standing. Further, there is a resistance to "rewarding" any slaveholder. Since slavery itself is universally illegal, slaveholders should no more be recompensed for giving up slaves than burglars should be paid to return their stolen goods. That said, there are situations in India where, primarily because the police are slow to respond to the crime of slavery, redemption is the only immediate and effective way to remove a person from danger.

A last resort

The lesson to be drawn from these examples is this: redeeming slaves has a role in the anti-slavery movement, but only when other actions have failed or are impossible. In one way it is the lesser of several evils. The greatest evil is enslavement. Paying a slaveholder or a middleman to free a slave is regrettable since freedom is a right and shouldn't need to be purchased. Yet, when there are situations where the authorities will not take action, where freedom is available only through redemption, and where enslaved people are suffering and threatened, then redemption may be the only immediate answer. A good case can be made both for and against redemption; a key criterion has to be that it be used only when it won't make things worse. It is but one tactic in an overall movement against slavery.

So, if redemption is a tactic, we have to ask: what are the other strategies that will bring people out of slavery? One effective method is to support partner organizations that raid workplaces where slaves are held, anywhere from quarries to carpet looms. Others help slaves to freedom by educating those in debt bondage about their rights and then helping them to act on those rights. One of the greatest obstacles to freedom is the inability or unwillingness of governments to enforce their own anti-slavery laws (even Sudan has a law against slavery). Through governments and the UN, an important way forward is to get police enforcing these laws; at times that requires asking countries like the U.S. to use their economic and diplomatic influence. The recent shift in the chocolate industry to work toward "slave-free" chocolate has shown how partnerships between businesses, unions, and human rights organizations can be formed to cut slavery out of a product chain, in this case slavery on cocoa farms in West Africa. After freedom comes the need for rehabilitation, through education, micro-credit, and other supports. Without rehabilitation people can fall back into slavery. At the end of the day the global anti-slavery movement is aiming for a situation where we are never forced to choose the "lesser of two evils," where liberation and rehabilitation are achieved as a right, not at a price.

10

Slave Redemption Increases Slavery in Sudan

Richard Miniter

Richard Miniter writes on subjects such as entrepreneurship, national politics, foreign affairs, and the environment. His articles have appeared in the New York Times, *the* Wall Street Journal, *and* Reader's Digest.

Sudan has been embroiled in a civil war between the Muslim North and the Christian South since the country gained its independence from Britain in 1956. The northern government in Khartoum encourages tribesmen to raid southern villages and abduct people, who are later sold in northern slave markets. To combat this problem, international organizations have been raising funds to purchase the freedom of slaves from slave traders, a practice known as slave redemption. Unfortunately, slave redemption increases the market value of slaves and encourages raiders to abduct more people to sell to slave redeemers. Eliminating the economic incentive for trading slaves rather than increasing it would be a more effective way to reduce slavery in Sudan.

S udan is Africa's largest country and its saddest case. Every ancient scourge lives here: war, famine, disease, pestilence, rape, mutilation, and slavery. Starvation and violence have cost some two million lives and displaced some five million people since 1983, according to Freedom House, a Washington-based human-rights organization. Robert A. Seiple, . . . the [former] president of World Vision United States, a relief and development group, has asked, "Is there a name for a million square miles of suffering? Yes. It is called Sudan." The United Nations and, indirectly, the United States government have since 1989 airlifted millions of tons of food to starving people in southern Sudan, the epicenter of a civil war. But it is the emergence of modern-day slavery that has seized the world's attention.

Entering southern Sudan, one sees the names of dozens of international agencies, nonprofit groups, and religious organizations plastered on Land Rovers and compound gates. There is no shortage here of good intentions. But far from the airstrips and offices, some Africans say that

Westerners are a large part of the problem: nearly everything the activists do makes matters worse. And the issues of slavery and starvation are joined in an unexpected and overlooked way that ensures the continued failure of humanitarian efforts. Still, the battle against slavery in Sudan can be won, if international officials have the sense to try a different, more hardheaded approach—one that does not include the much-publicized practice of redeeming slaves for money.

Documenting the problem

The evil of slavery, which had been virtually eliminated by the British during the First World War, returned to Sudan in 1989, when the fundamentalist political party known as the National Islamic Front took control of the government in Khartoum and decided to arm Baggara tribesmen so that they could fight the rebellious Christian tribes of the south in Sudan's widening civil war. That war, which has raged intermittently ever since the country gained independence from Britain, in 1956, pits the educated, technologically superior Muslim north against the poor, undeveloped, and populous Christian and animist south. The Baggara are a Muslim people who in the past enslaved their neighbors, the cattle-herding Dinkas. Re-armed, the Baggara resumed the slave raids that the British had ended. They were aided and encouraged by the Khartoum government, which supplied auxiliary troops, known as the Popular Defence Forces, and also provided horses, guns, and ammunition. The government allowed slave markets to open in Khartoum, Juba, Wau, and other cities it controlled. Thousands of Dinkas, mostly women and children, have been seized in raids and taken north on foot or by train, over hundreds of miles of rocky, arid wasteland, to be sold, sometimes for as little as $15 apiece. Family members are often separated as they are parceled out to different buyers. Their Muslim owners, who do not speak the slaves' language, consider it a traditional right to enslave southerners; their word for a southern tribesman, abd, is synonymous with "slave." The slaves have been put to work as cooks, maids, field hands, and concubines. Some teenage males have been forcibly circumcised; a number of females have been ritually mutilated. Many are fed and kept like cattle, often sleeping beside livestock that their owners consider far more valuable. Like cattle, they are branded, sometimes just below the eye, with the Arabic name of their owner.

> *The issues of slavery and starvation . . . [ensure] the continued failure of humanitarian efforts.*

By the early 1990s reports of slavery's return began trickling out of Bahr al Ghazal, a Dinka region in southern Sudan, to relief and development groups helping Sudanese refugees in Uganda and Kenya. At first the reports were hard to believe, and aid workers accepted the Sudanese government's adamant denials. But new eyewitnesses kept coming forward. If their reports were true, aid workers wondered, how could the situation be brought to the world's attention?

The answer was provided by John Eibner, an official at Christian Solidarity International [CSI], a group based in Zurich [Switzerland] that had been founded in 1977 to fight the persecution of Christians and religious minorities in the Soviet Union and elsewhere. CSI, now also dedicated to assisting victims of war and famine, has played a major role in shaping the response to slavery in Sudan. In May of 1995, defying the Sudanese government, Eibner chartered a plane and flew deep into Sudan's "no go" area. There he met dozens of Dinka mothers who told him about their abducted children. He could no longer doubt that the resurgence of slavery was real.

Upon his return to Switzerland, Eibner persuaded reporters from around the world to make the dangerous and illegal trek into Sudan to document the slave trade. He led journalists from *The Baltimore Sun* and other newspapers to the open-air slave markets. "Witness to Slavery," a series that the *Sun* published in June of 1996, shocked Western officials and human-rights advocates. The [Bill] Clinton Administration imposed comprehensive trade and economic sanctions on Sudan in 1997. Still, economic leverage was limited: all direct U.S. aid to Sudan had been cut off years earlier, owing to the 1989 coup d'etat. In 1993 the United States had added Sudan to the list of countries it believes sponsor terrorism, further reducing the prospects for international aid. Other industrialized nations publicly condemned the Sudanese government's tolerance of slavery. Not surprisingly, world outrage did nothing to diminish it.

I began to realize that there was also the potential [in slave redemption] for abuse.

How widespread is slavery in Sudan? It must be said that hard numbers of the sort Americans are accustomed to do not exist. There is no question that scores of raids occur every year, and many thousands of people now live in captivity. There are many accurate local statistics: villages keep fairly complete lists of their people who have been killed or captured. But no reliable national data exist to provide a complete picture of the crisis. The chaos of civil war makes comprehensive data collection difficult, and only sporadically do the village reports reach county governments, or county lists reach the rebel command in Nairobi. In some regions, such as the Nuba Mountains and Darfur, records have been destroyed in the intense fighting or are no longer kept. Steven Wondu, the Washington representative of the rebels' Sudanese People's Liberation Army, offered 20,000 as a very rough estimate of the number of slaves in Sudan. Whatever the precise figure, local reports and the personal experience of Western aid workers and journalists are sufficient to conclude that slavery is a persistent threat.

John Eibner came up with the idea of Westerners' buying back slaves, building on a practice already used by local people. As Eibner relates, "On previous visits we heard about the efforts of local people to get their loved ones out of bondage through a retrieval mechanism that had been established as part of a local Dinka-Arab peace agreement, which was signed in 1991." By the fall of 1995 Christian Solidarity International was in the business of buying slaves in large batches and setting them free. The organization called the process "slave redemption."

Community efforts

[Throughout 1998 and 1999] raising money for slave redemption [became] a focus of well-intentioned activity in many public schools and evangelical churches. In these supposedly apathetic times the plight of Sudanese slaves has inspired countless institutions and community groups across the United States, Canada, and Western Europe. Dozens of nonprofit agencies, relief groups, and missionary organizations are raising hundreds of thousands of dollars a year for "freedom funds."

Barbara Vogel's fifth-grade class at the Highline Community School, in Aurora, Colorado, was the first public school class to raise money for slave redemptions. The effort began in February of [1998], when Vogel read her students an article from *The Rocky Mountain News* about the plight of Sudanese slaves. "Nothing hit my kids like this did," Vogel told me recently. "They cried. They all agreed we had to do something." By selling lemonade, T-shirts, and old toys, the Aurora students raised more than $1,000 within the year. Media attention, including a feature on the CBS Evening News, brought in donations from across the country, ultimately totaling more than $50,000. Many other schools have followed Vogel's lead, including the Damascus Middle School, in Oregon, where fifth-, sixth-, and seventh-graders raised $2,500 on their own.

Christian Solidarity International, which says it has freed almost 8,000 slaves since 1995, is by far the largest of about a dozen groups that buy slaves out of bondage. In what was billed as the largest single slave redemption to date, in January of [1999] CSI bought 1,050 slaves for the equivalent (in Sudanese pounds) of $52,500—$50 each. In April [1999], CSI broke its record, freeing 1,783 slaves. Meanwhile, Christian Solidarity Worldwide, a London-based group headed by Baroness Caroline Cox, redeemed 325 slaves. Cox, a member of the House of Lords, has attracted her own following, including a number of donors in the United States.

James Jacobson, at the time the vice-president of the National Right to Read Foundation, a literacy group based in The Plains, Virginia, became CSI's Washington representative in November of 1995. At first he was a loyal supporter of slave redemption. During the next few years CSI was beset by internal differences that resulted in the breakaway of the British, Austrian, and American offices, among others. The American operation achieved independence [in 1998], as Christian Freedom International, with James Jacobson at its head. Vowing to pursue the same objectives as CSI, but handicapped by his lack of firsthand experience of Sudan, Jacobson made a trip to the war zone. He traveled to remote villages and met former slaves who were scarred from beatings. "I felt satisfied that slavery was real," he said, "but I began to realize that there was also the potential [in slave redemption] for abuse." As media reports and the number of redemptions by an increasing assortment of groups multiplied rapidly, so did Jacobson's doubts and fears.

Subsequent visits to Sudan gradually revealed what Jacobson regarded as the consequences of good intentions gone awry, and after his most recent visit to Sudan, on which I accompanied him, he has reluctantly turned away from slave redemption as a tactic. Though his organization is still actively involved in Sudan, shipping clothing, tools, and school supplies, Jacobson identifies three problems with current humanitarian efforts there. First, the financial incentives of slave redemption are so powerful in Sudan, one of the world's poorest nations, that they encourage the taking of slaves. Second, even when the incentives don't promote slavery, they can promote hoaxes. Third, the way the United Nations distributes food acts as a magnet for slave raiders.

Encouraging the slave trade

The per capita income in Sudan, according to Sudanese embassy estimates, is about $500 a year. In the war-torn south it is much less. A small amount of money injected from the outside can create a powerful dynamic. Selling slaves back to their families for $50 to $100 each—with the financial assistance of Westerners—is far more profitable than selling them for about $15 in the northern slave markets. "We've made slavery more profitable than narcotics," Jacobson says. Recently I asked Manase Lomole Waya, who runs Humanitarian Assistance for South Sudan, a group based in Nairobi, what he thought about slave-redemption efforts. "We welcome them for exposing the agony of our people to the world," he said. "That part is good. But giving the money to the slave traders only encourages the trade. It is wrong and must stop. Where does the money go? It goes to the raiders to buy more guns, raid more villages, put more shillings in their pockets. It is a vicious circle."

What seems to have kept the slave business afloat is the high prices paid by the slave redeemers.

Slave redeemers enrich every element of the trade: raiders, owners, and traders. Once, the main objective of roving militias and Baggara raiders was simply war booty: goats, cattle, and other valuables, with a few slaves taken to make a little extra money on the side. The price of a slave rose to $300, however, and slaves became the focus of the raids. By the mid-nineties supply had outpaced demand, and prices began to fall—to about $100 in 1995 and then to $15 in 1997. Plunging prices threatened to put the traders out of business: paying and arming raiders, and feeding and watering their horses in a dry region, is very expensive.

What seems to have kept the slave business afloat is the high prices paid by the slave redeemers. Though redemption prices also fell, they stayed far above the $15 paid in slave markets. CSI, according to its publications, paid the equivalent of about $100 for each freed slave from 1995 to 1997 and since then has paid about $50. In effect the redeemers are keeping prices high and creating a powerful incentive for raids.

Some slave-redemption proponents argue that they must pay a risk premium—a sum sufficient to encourage dealers to bring slaves back to the south. CSI suggests that the premium is necessary to cover the costs of food, water, and armed guards to transport the slaves. "Traders incur substantial costs and serious risks for their own security," a CSI report from October of 1997 concludes. Fair enough—but no matter how the price for redeemed slaves is justified, the simple fact is that redemption makes the trade much more lucrative.

Another indication that slave redemption has spurred raids is that the size of a typical raiding party has grown from roughly 400 attackers in 1995 to more than 2,500 [in 1999], according to figures compiled by the Sudanese Relief and Rehabilitation Association, the rebels' civilian arm. Why, in an era of falling prices, did the raiders more than sextuple their overhead? To garner more of the slave redeemers' bounty. It seems certain that without redemption, the raiding parties would have diminished.

A number of Dinka leaders, along with Macram Gassis, one of Sudan's eleven Catholic bishops, strongly support slave redemption, and some seek to make CSI the sole redeemer. However, the Dinkas I spoke with, all of whom live in villages that have been victimized by the raiders, strongly oppose redemption altogether on the grounds that it promotes raids. In February [1999] the Akoch Payam settlement was attacked by more than 2,500 horsemen and foot soldiers. Thirty-six people were killed and another seventy were taken away as slaves (along with food and thousands of animals). "Redemption is not the solution," Longar Awic Ayuel, Akoch's executive chief, told me a few days after the raid. "It means that you are encouraging the raiders."

The official spokesman for the Akoch district government, Adelino Rip Goc, emphatically agreed with Ayuel. "It is common sense not to pay the men who kill your father and steal your brother, or they will return," he said. "I don't know why the redeemers do such a thing."

As I spoke with Goc, a crowd of villagers encircled us. Does anyone here support slave redemption? I asked. No one did. One man said that I should talk to Machar Malok Machar. In a previous raid on Akoch, Machar was captured and marched into the desert. Before sunrise on the second day he crawled away and hid. He waited for hours until the Muslim slave raiders departed. Then he walked home, with his hands still tied behind his back, to find his wife and family missing, his hut burned, his cattle and goats gone. After I heard his story, I asked him about slave redemption. "It is bad," he said. "They do these terrible things to put shillings in their pockets. They are crazy for the money. Why would you give it to them?"

Redemption reduces any incentive for owners to set slaves free.

A number of human-rights organizations concerned with Sudan are also skeptical of slave redemption and its unintended consequences. UNICEF, the United Nations Children's Fund, has called the practice "intolerable," because "the buy-back program implicitly accepts that human beings may be bought and sold," as Paul Lewis, a reporter for *The New York Times*, explains. "This could also encourage slave-taking for profit." Reed Brody, the advocacy director for Human Rights Watch, says that although redemption is understandably welcomed by many abductees and their families, it poses a "real danger of fueling a market in human beings." To date neither organization has issued an official report condemning slave redemption.

Redemption reduces any incentive for owners to set slaves free. Prior to 1995 about 10 percent of slaves, mostly old women and small children, were allowed to escape or even told to go home, because they cost too much to feed; some of the younger female slaves were let go because they made the owners' wives jealous. Though this meant a dangerous and lonely trek across the desert for the manumitted slaves, it helped to keep the size of the slave population in check. Today many northerners consider their slaves an investment. Acutely aware of the redemption money available, they sell their human chattels to middlemen, who take the slaves south.

Redemption also rewards slave traders. Many entrepreneurs who sold a variety of contraband goods prior to 1995 now deal solely in slaves. It is more profitable. As in many businesses, the man in the middle stands to make the most money. Raiders may earn $5 to $15 per slave; traders can earn several times as much. The trader, that vital link, is the worst person to enrich. Without him the typical raider has no market for his captives—he can hardly resell them to their families, and he has no personal access to buyers in the north. In contrast, the trader moves easily between the two worlds. Thanks to the redeemers, who treat them as business partners, traders are richer than ever and, indeed, enjoy a measure of legitimacy as the linchpin of the redemption chain. This is not the result that the redeemers intended.

Incentives for hoaxes

The money available to redeem slaves has attracted the attention of people other than "legitimate" traders. No one can say how widespread slave-redemption hoaxes may be, though even John Eibner concedes the possibility of fraud: "I have at times refused to cooperate with people who have asked CSI to provide money for slave redemption when I have not been convinced that sound ethical standards are being strictly adhered to," he says. Eibner believes that he has adequate safeguards in place, including a determined effort to match the names of retrieved slaves with those on local lists of abductees.

I witnessed an attempted slave redemption that was unquestionably problematic during a recent visit to Nyamlell, a large settlement about fifty miles south of the Bahr al Arab River, in southern Sudan. Nyamlell has been the location of many slave redemptions covered by the U.S. media. The night before my visit officials from the local branch of the Sudanese Relief and Rehabilitation Association [SRRA] in Lokichokio, Kenya, asked for a meeting with James Jacobson, who had been hoping to redeem the slaves in Nyamlell. After half an hour of small talk the officials got down to business. "How much money are you bringing for slave redemption?"

"Four thousand dollars," Jacobson said.

"Ah, that is very helpful. There are forty slave children to be redeemed."

"Forty children? That would be a hundred dollars each. Don't other groups pay fifty dollars each?"

"No. Everyone pays a hundred."

"What about Christian Solidarity International?"

"Ah, they are different. They buy in much larger quantities."

Though the overwhelming majority of rebel officials are honest, it would be unsurprising if a few used their access to well-intentioned redeemers and desperately poor village leaders to make money. One scam is said to work as follows. Corrupt officials set themselves up as bankers and insist that redeemers exchange their dollars for Sudanese pounds, a nearly worthless currency. (People in the south almost always use Ugandan and Kenyan shillings or U.S. dollars.) The officials arrange by radio to have some villagers play slaves and some play slave-sellers, and when the redeemers arrive, the Sudanese pounds are used to free the slaves. When the redeemers are gone, the pounds are turned back over to the corrupt officials, who hand out a few dollars in return. Most of the dollars stay with the officials, who now also have the Sudanese pounds with which to play banker again.

Jacobson exchanged no money, but two mid-level SRRA officials insisted on accompanying him and me to Nyamlell. When we landed on the dirt runway, a local commissioner named Alev Akechak Jok met our plane. He refused to make eye contact with the SRRA officials, and was adamant about meeting privately with Jacobson and me. A guard with an AK-47 barred the SRRA officials from joining us in the compound. The commissioner offered tea and an admission: "There are no slaves here for you to buy." He was happy to elaborate on the problem of slave raids—a real menace in his part of the world—but he would not say why there was no one in Nyamlell to be redeemed, only repeating that there was no one. Hadn't the SRRA radioed his village the previous day and learned that there were forty children to be freed? He shook his head no.

As we returned to the airstrip, the SRRA officials rejoined us. One said that he had just found a trader and ten children to be redeemed. Jok suddenly became angry and pulled me aside. The officials could not hear us over the whirling propeller. "You must leave now!" he demanded. Are the children slaves? I asked. "No," he said, "they are the children of the village. We do not want you to do this thing. We are Christian people. We do not want the world to turn its face from us." Jok has since been removed from his post, probably in retaliation for his honesty.

As Jok's example suggests, honest villagers often refuse to play along. A few days before the incident in Nyamlell, Steven Wondu, of the Sudanese People's Liberation Army, and Caroline Cox waited for two days in the district of Turalei for some traders who were supposed to arrive with slaves to redeem. None came. The village leaders repeatedly told Cox and the journalists she had brought along that there had been no slave raids in Turalei for more than a year, and that there was no one to redeem. Cox, with the dejected reporters, flew out on the morning of the third day. "Why are you disappointed?" Wondu asked.

Creating a target

Lokichokio, just inside the Kenyan border with Sudan, is a settlement that has grown up around relief efforts. It is the site of a UN-controlled airstrip and the local headquarters of the UN's World Food Program. From Loki, as it is called, giant Hercules cargo planes carry tons of food and medicine to distant airstrips where the hungry wait in the shade of mud huts.

The World Food Program, which here takes the form of Operation Lifeline Sudan, has made it very easy for the Sudanese government to coordinate slave raids and food drops. Before every airlift of food UN officials notify Khartoum—whose forces have largely created the famine, in pursuance of a policy of starving the southerners into submission—exactly where and when they plan to deposit the food. No relief planes are allowed to leave the ground without Khartoum's explicit permission. Not surprisingly, in Bahr al Ghazal, Khartoum-backed raiders often arrive in time to seize the shipment and enslave enough locals to carry it. "That's the cycle," one cynical pilot says. I encountered the aftermath of just such an episode in the village of Akoch.

The economic rewards for slave trading must be eliminated.

To appreciate how a policy with such counterproductive consequences can be maintained, one must understand the atmosphere of utter bureaucratic indifference in Lokichokio. After the attack on Akoch, several family members brought out a gravely wounded woman named Anchor Ring, a grandmother of perhaps sixty, and put her under the wing of our plane. A horseman had slashed her head with a machete, leaving a wound deep enough to expose the yellow membrane surrounding her brain. Could we take her to the hospital in Loki? her family asked. The plane was half empty. The pilot radioed Loki's UN compound. The response came in the form of a question: "Does she have a valid passport and visa for travel into Kenya?" We were in rebel-held land, hundreds of miles from electric power, running water, or government offices. "No papers?" the voice said. "Tell her the hospital is full."

Denial and deflection

In the course of many conversations I have had with them, the supporters of slave redemption have been unwilling to address the issue of perverse incentives directly. They have countered obliquely with three arguments: slave redemption draws public attention to the tragedy in Sudan; it chips away at the slave trade one person at a time; and it ends the personal suffering of slaves and their families.

Publicity is perhaps the most frequently cited rationale for slave redemption. Certainly the on-camera manumission of a modern-day slave presents a powerful image for broadcast television. But surely the shocking reports of slave raids and the painful stories of former slaves are dramatic enough in themselves to hold the public's attention. Redemption alone doesn't provide any special public-relations benefit—and it may contain the seeds of a public-relations disaster. Of course, it is a powerful fundraising tool. I do not believe that any of the redemption groups have other than noble motives; but the "success" of slave redemption may blind some activists to its unintended consequences.

Does redemption chip away at slavery? Undeniably, individual slaves have been given their freedom. But as the raiding parties have grown in size, the number of slaves taken has also grown. Sitting beneath color charts on food production and hand-drawn spreadsheets quantifying the deaths, injuries, and stolen livestock in southern Sudan, Erib Gaetano Felix, an SRRA statistician, observes matter-of-factly that slave raids have "gotten much worse every year since 1995."

Anti-slavery activists, including Michael Horowitz, of the Hudson Institute, and Charles Jacobs, of the American Anti-Slavery Group, explain the increase in slave-taking since 1995 in terms of the growing intensity of the Sudanese war. But although war is the context for the slave trade, it cannot be the main cause. The Khartoum government, which promotes the trade, has been retreating. Since 1995 the rebels, often driving captured government trucks and tanks, have seized an increasing share of Bahr al Ghazal, where most raids take place. So why is slave-taking on the rise? The raiders are essentially privateers; if the raids did not pay for themselves, the raiders would stay home. That is why they take slaves and other booty, while the main government force focuses on the destruction of strategic assets. The raiders pose a continuing threat because their bands, though sizable, are still small enough to find openings in the rebels' lines. And high prices make the risk worthwhile.

What about the humanitarian case for redemption? Activists screen emotional videos of former slaves and ask viewers to imagine that a spouse or a child had been enslaved. Wouldn't they pay for redemption? "When you personalize it like that, the answer is obvious," an abolitionist pastor told *The Oregonian*. But public policy requires a focus on the larger interest. With good reason, the U.S. government does not negotiate with terrorists or pay ransom to kidnappers. Presented with this argument, activists simply sidestep it. Michael Horowitz says, "[Redemption] may not be the answer to the problem, but it is the answer to many mothers' prayers."

A policy that works

Deciding that it is better not to buy individuals their freedom needn't mean turning our backs on the people of Sudan. But the economic rewards for slave trading must be eliminated.

The United Nations and the U.S. government should require that all organizations, governmental and nongovernmental, forswear slave redemption as a condition of working in Sudan. Operation Lifeline Sudan must be reformed or suspended so that it does not indirectly aid the Khartoum government. The UN should cease notifying Khartoum about the timing and cargo of its flights.

James Jacobson's organization, confronting redemption's perverse incentives, has decided to stop redeeming slaves. Jacobson has mailed letters to more than 6,000 donors, offering to return their money or to redirect it to other humanitarian efforts. Those other efforts could include some unorthodox approaches to fighting slavery in Sudan. One idea is the provision of used trucks and jeeps. Slave raiders arrive on horseback; owing to the flat, treeless landscape, they can be seen for miles. "With trucks you can head off the raiders and stop them from taking slaves, or you can chase after them and rescue people," Jacobson explains.

He also wants to put slave rescuers on salary. The rescuers could be recruited from the nomadic Rizeiqat tribe, whose members move freely in the north and even now often help to find enslaved people in exchange for the right to water their cattle on Dinka land. The Rizeiqat could be sent north with lists of people known to have been enslaved. Most hamlets in Bahr al Ghazal keep detailed lists of the missing, more than a few of which I have seen. These lists give the full name of each abducted person, his or her age, and the approximate date of capture. The lists could be collected and consolidated into a database. A rescuer who found a person on the list could help him or her to break out of captivity and return home. This would cut out the middlemen who make the slave trade possible. It would also curb hoaxes.

Policymakers, meanwhile, should focus their attention on what antislavery activists call the "train of death." This train, which runs between Khartoum and the city of Wau, a southern stronghold of the government, is the primary means of transport used by the slave raiders. Without it they would not be able to transport large numbers of slaves north or provide enough water for their horses. Virtually all raids occur within a two-day ride of the rail line. Severing that rail link would at a stroke curtail slavery in Sudan. But the rebels lack the tools—and outside governments lack the will.

Crafting a successful abolitionist foreign policy has never been easy, as the long British experience suggests. Beginning in the 1820s, the British sought to end slavery throughout their empire. With their powerful army and navy they shut down most of the slave markets in the African colonies within a decade. Yet pockets of slavery kept emerging for another hundred years. Throughout the nineteenth century the British government dispatched soldiers to kill or disarm slave raiders, and sent warships to crush the warlords who sheltered slave traders. Not until the first decades of this century did their campaign succeed. Even so, they had to remain vigilant lest slavery break out again. "If the colonial government were standing for election, I would vote for them," a Nairobi schoolmaster told me recently. "They gave us more than sacks of grain and kind words." One does not need to accept this wistful vote for colonialism to take the point that fighting slavery is not a task for sentimentalists.

11

Reparations Should Be Paid to Descendants of African American Slaves

Randall Robinson

Randall Robinson is founder and president of the TransAfrica Forum, a think tank in Washington, D.C., and author of The Debt: What America Owes to Blacks, *from which this viewpoint is excerpted.*

The United States profited enormously from the unpaid labor of black slaves for 246 years. The practice of slavery in America created a social atmosphere rife with racism and an economic disparity between whites and blacks that remains today. This economic inequality perpetuates slavery's legacy of racism and prevents blacks from reaching their full potential. These problems can only be solved when the U.S. government recognizes how destructive the institution of slavery has been to the African American community and compensates the descendants of slaves accordingly. The black community must unite to fight for the reparations that should have been paid to their ancestors.

On January 5, 1993, Congressman John Conyers, a black Democrat from Detroit, introduced in Congress a bill to "acknowledge the fundamental injustice, cruelty, brutality, and inhumanity of slavery in the United States and the 13 American colonies between 1619 and 1865 and to establish a commission to examine the institution of slavery, subsequent *de jure* and *de facto* racial and economic discrimination against African Americans, and the impact of these forces on living African Americans, to make recommendations to the Congress on appropriate remedies, and for other purposes."

The bill, which did not ask for reparations for the descendants of slaves but merely a commission to study the effects of slavery, won from the 435-member U.S. House of Representatives only 28 cosponsors, 18 of whom were black.

The measure was referred to the House Committee on the Judiciary and from there to the House Subcommittee on Civil and Constitutional Rights. The bill has never made it out of committee. . . .

[And yet,] if African Americans will not be compensated for the massive wrongs and social injuries inflicted upon them by their government, during and after slavery, then there is *no* chance that America can solve its racial problems—if solving these problems means, as I believe it must, closing the yawning economic gap between blacks and whites in this country. The gap was opened by the 246-year practice of slavery. It has been resolutely nurtured since in law and public behavior. It has now ossified. It is structural. Its framing beams are disguised only by the counterfeit manners of a hypocritical governing class.

The United States government provided no compensation to the victims of slavery.

For twelve years Nazi Germany inflicted horrors upon European Jews. And Germany paid. It paid Jews individually. It paid the state of Israel. For two and a half centuries, Europe and America inflicted unimaginable horrors upon Africa and its people. Europe not only paid nothing to Africa in compensation, but followed the slave trade with the remapping of Africa for further European economic exploitation. (European governments have yet even to accede to Africa's request for the return of Africa's art treasures looted along with its natural resources during the century-long colonial era.)

While President [Abraham] Lincoln supported a plan during the Civil War to compensate slave owners for their loss of "property," his successor, Andrew Johnson, vetoed legislation that would have provided compensation to ex-slaves.

Under the Southern Homestead Act, ex-slaves were given six months to purchase land at reasonably low rates without competition from white southerners and northern investors. But, owing to their destitution, few ex-slaves were able to take advantage of the homesteading program. The largest number that did were concentrated in Florida, numbering little more than three thousand. The soil was generally poor and unsuitable for farming purposes. In any case, the ex-slaves had no money on which to subsist for months while waiting for crops, or the scantest wherewithal to purchase the most elementary farming implements. The program failed. In sum, the United States government provided no compensation to the victims of slavery.

Why reparations are critical

Perhaps I should say a bit here about why the question of reparations is critical to finding a solution to our race problems.

This question—and how blacks gather to pose it—is a good measure of our psychological readiness as a community to pull ourselves abreast here at home and around the world. I say this because no outside community can be more interested in solving our problems than we. [Harvard Law professor] Derrick Bell suggested in his review of [Boris] Bittker's book

[*The Case for Black Reparations*] that the white power structure would never support reparations because to do so would operate against its interests. I believe Bell is right in that view. The initiative must come from blacks, broadly, widely, implacably.

But what exactly will black enthusiasm, or lack thereof, measure? There is no linear solution to any of our problems, for our problems are not merely technical in nature. By now, after 380 years of unrelenting psychological abuse, the biggest part of our problem is inside us: in how we have come to see ourselves, in our damaged capacity to validate a course for ourselves without outside approval.

The issue here is not whether or not we can, or will, win reparations. The issue rather is whether we will fight for reparations, because we have decided for ourselves that they are our due. In 1915, into the sharp teeth of southern Jim Crow hostility, Cornelius J. Jones filed a lawsuit against the United States Department of the Treasury in an attempt to recover sixty-eight million dollars for former slaves. He argued that, through a federal tax placed on raw cotton, the federal government had benefited financially from the sale of cotton that slave labor had produced, and for which the black men, women, and children who had produced the cotton had not been paid. Jones's was a straightforward proposition. The monetary value of slaves' labor, which he estimated to be sixty-eight million dollars, had been appropriated by the United States government. A debt existed. It had to be paid to the, by then, ex-slaves or their heirs.

The United States government and white society generally have opted to deal with this debt *by forgetting that it is owed.*

Where was the money?

A federal appeals court held that the United States could not be sued without its consent and dismissed the so-called Cotton Tax case. But the court never addressed Cornelius J. Jones's question about the federal government's appropriation of property—the labor of blacks who had worked the cotton fields—that had never been compensated.

The value of their labor

Let me try to drive the point home here: through keloids of suffering, through coarse veils of damaged self-belief, lost direction, misplaced compass, shit-faced resignation, racial transmutation, black people worked long, hard, killing days, years, centuries—and they were never *paid*. The value of their labor went into others' pockets—plantation owners, northern entrepreneurs, state treasuries, the United States government.

Where was the money?

Where *is* the money?

There is a debt here.

I know of no statute of limitations either legally or morally that would extinguish it. Financial quantities are nearly as indestructible as matter. Take away here, add there, interest compounding annually, over the years, over the whole of the twentieth century.

Where is the money?

Jews have asked this question of countries and banks and corporations and collectors and any who had been discovered at the end of the slimy line holding in secret places the gold, the art, the money that was the rightful property of European Jews before the Nazi terror. Jews have demanded what was their due and received a fair measure of it. . . .

Successful claims for reparations

After World War I the allies made successful claims against Germany, as would Jews after World War II. The Poles also laid claims against the Germans after being used by the Nazis during the Second World War as slave labor. Japanese-Americans recovered from the United States government. The Inuit recovered from the Canadian government. Aborigines recovered money and large areas of land from the Australian government. Korean women, forced into prostitution by Japan during World War II, were compensated as well.

According to [lawyer and activist] Dudley Thompson, international law in this area is replete with precedents.

> Not only is there a moral debt but there is clearly established precedence in law based on the principle of unjust enrichment. In law if a party unlawfully enriches himself by wrongful acts against another, then the party so wronged is entitled to recompense. There have been some 15 cases in which the highest tribunals including the International Court at the Hague have awarded large sums as reparations based on this law.

Only in the case of black people have the claims, the claimants, the crime, the law, the precedents, the awful contemporary social consequences all been roundly ignored. The thinking must be that the case that cannot be substantively answered is best not acknowledged at all. Hence, the United States government and white society generally have opted to deal with this *debt* by forgetting that it is owed. The crime—246 years of an enterprise murderous both of a people and their culture—is so unprecedentedly massive that it would require some form of collective insanity not to see it and its living victims.

The life and responsibilities of a society or nation are not circumscribed by the life spans of its mortal constituents.

But still many, if not most, whites cannot or will not see it (a behavior that is accommodated by all too many uncomplaining blacks). This studied white blindness may be a modern variant of a sight condition that afflicted their slaveholding forebears who concocted something called *drapetomania*, the so-called mental disorder that slaveholders seriously believed caused blacks to run away to freedom. America accepts responsibility for little that goes wrong in the world, least of all the contemporary plight of black Americans. And until America can be made to do so, it is hard to see how we can progress significantly in our race relations. . . .

Shouldering the responsibilities of a younger America

Well before the birth of our country, Europe and the eventual United States perpetrated a heinous wrong against the peoples of Africa—and sustained and benefited from the wrong for centuries. Europe followed the grab of Africa's people with the rape, through colonial occupation, of Africa's material resources. America followed slavery with more than a hundred combined years of legal racial segregation and legal racial discrimination of one variety or another. In 1965, after nearly 350 years of legal racial suppression, the United States enacted the *Voting Rights Act* and, virtually simultaneously, began to walk away from the social wreckage that centuries of white hegemony had wrought. The country then began to rub itself with the memory-emptying salve of contemporaneousness. (If the wrong did not *just* occur, it did not occur at all in a way that would render the living responsible.)

A large debt is owed by America to the descendants of America's slaves.

But when the black living suffer real and current consequences as a result of wrongs committed by a younger America, then contemporary America must be caused to shoulder responsibility for those wrongs until such wrongs have been adequately compensated and righted. The life and responsibilities of a society or nation are not circumscribed by the life spans of its mortal constituents. Social rights, wrongs, obligations, and responsibilities flow eternal.

There are many ways to begin righting America's massive wrong, some of which you must already have inferred. But let there be no doubt, it will require great resources and decades of national fortitude to resolve economic and social disparities so long in the making.

Habit is the enemy. For whites and blacks have made a habit now, beyond the long era of legal discrimination, of seeing each other (the only way they can remember seeing each other) in a certain relation of economic and social inequality.

American capitalism, which starts each child where its parents left off is not a fair system. This is particularly the case for African Americans, whose general economic starting points have been rearmost in our society because of slavery and its long racialist aftermath. American slaves for two and a half centuries saw taken from them not just their freedom but the inestimable economic value of their labor as well, which, were it a line item in today's gross national product report, would undoubtedly run into the billions of dollars. Whether the monetary obligation is legally enforceable or not, a large debt is owed by America to the descendants of America's slaves.

Here too, habit has become our enemy, for America has made an art form by now of grinding its past deeds, no matter how despicable, into mere ephemera. African Americans, unfortunately, have accommodated this habit of American amnesia all too well. It would behoove African Americans to remember that history forgets, first, those who forget themselves. To do what is necessary to accomplish anything approaching psychic and economic parity in the next half century will not only require a fundamental attitude shift in American thinking but massive amounts of money as well. Before the country in general can be made to understand, African Americans themselves must come to understand that this demand is not for charity. It is simply for what they are *owed* on a debt that is old but compellingly obvious and valid still.

Even the *making* of a well-reasoned case for restitution will do wonders for the spirit of African Americans. It will cause them at long last to understand the genesis of their dilemma by gathering, as have all other groups, all of their history—before, during and after slavery—into one story of themselves. To hold the story fast to their breast. To make of it, over time, a sacred text. And from it, to explain themselves to themselves and to their heirs. Tall again, as they had been long, long ago.

12

Reparations Should Not Be Paid to Descendants of African American Slaves

Karl Zinsmeister

Karl Zinsmeister is the editor-in-chief of the American Enterprise, *a monthly journal of politics, business, and culture.*

Paying reparations to the decendants of African American slaves would not right the wrong of slavery because slaves and those who benefited from slavery are no longer living. Sorting out who should receive reparations and who should pay them is too complicated, now that the identities of oppressors and the oppressed have been blurred through racial mixing. Moreover, Americans have tried to compensate for slavery through greater social assistance for African Americans, such as increased spending on social programs combating poverty and on affirmative action. On the whole, blacks have thrived in America and enjoy a better quality of life in the United States than they would have if they had been born in Africa.

The activist campaign demanding payment of "slavery reparations" to today's black Americans probably strikes some readers as too far-fetched to take seriously. Better stop and look afresh. I myself realized that the concept had moved beyond faculty lounges, radical salons, and afro-centric pamphlets and into the realm of serious political struggle when I looked over the roster of a legal group convened to plot practical strategy for winning such compensation. It included not only Dream Teamer Johnny Cochran, Harvard Law School professor Charles Ogletree, and other ideologically predictable backers, but also one Richard J. Scruggs.

Scruggs is a white Mississippi trial lawyer with a single interest: causes which have a good chance of winning him lots of money. He is in the process of collecting billions of dollars (literally) for his part in the 1998 tobacco settlement. He is next trying to shake down HMOs and other un-popular businesses with the threat of legal action. He has his finger in dozens of other polemicized class-action suits. Scruggs also happens to be the brother-in-law of Republican Senator Trent Lott. When legal vultures like Scruggs, Dennis Sweet (hyper rich from Fen-phen diet pill suits), and class-action specialists Willie Gary and Alexander Pires begin to circle— they're all currently members of a "Reparations Assessment Group" which has both government and major corporations in its sights—some juicy carcass is usually about to be picked clean.

Since both slaves and slave owners are no longer with us, compensation is beyond our reach.

There are other hints that the push for payments to slave descendants is gaining momentum. [Throughout 2000 and 2001], a dozen big-city councils have passed resolutions calling on the federal government to investigate reparations payments. Representative John Conyers has a bill in Congress that would require that. Representative Tony Hall, a white born-again Christian, is pushing a different proposal that would take up reparations; Republican congressman J.C. Watts has expressed guarded support. [As of this printing these bills are pending.] Quasi-conservative *Washington Post* columnist Charles Krauthammer wrote a column in April [2001] proposing to give African-American families a lump sum of $50,000 each.

Among blacks on the street, meanwhile, interest in reparations is shifting from pipe dream to popular demand. When I was in Dallas [in 2000], I heard hortatory ads by pro-reparations groups on black radio stations. Longstanding activist calls for black taxpayers to deduct "slavery credits" from their tax payments are being heeded by more African Americans. The IRS field office responsible for the region stretching just from northern Virginia to Delaware received 500 tax returns claiming such a credit (illegitimately) [in 2000]. "We're not talking about welfare. We're talking about back pay," is how the executive editor of *Ebony* magazine now describes reparations. Overall, polls show that most black Americans support having the government make slavery-restitution payments—in some surveys by considerably more than two-to-one.

This subject is not going to just quietly go away, as many Americans probably wish it would. The question must be faced. Are there merits to the case for slavery reparations?

A good idea whose time has gone

I myself would characterize reparations as a good idea whose time has come and long since gone. In the years leading up to the Civil War there were various proposals for ending slavery through government payments. Lincoln called for federal compensation to states according to the number of slaves they emancipated. A portion of these payments could have been used to help the freed blacks establish themselves in a new life. Unfortunately, nothing came of this.

After financial dickering gave way to war, Union General William Sherman issued his famous field order decreeing that all freed slaves should be issued a mule and forty acres of land appropriated from plantation owners. But this was later countermanded. Much to the frustration of Republicans, new President Andrew Johnson vetoed such payments.

The result—a miserable one for blacks and for our nation—was that slaves, though liberated, were not provided any resources to help them transform themselves into self-supporting Americans. The "new Negro," [famous black abolitionist] Frederick Douglass wrote, "had neither money, property, nor friends. He was free from the old plantation, but he had nothing but the dusty road under his feet. . . . He was turned loose naked, hungry, and destitute to the open sky."

If cash had been spent as it should have been in the 1850s or '60s on reparations to slaves and indemnities to slaveowners, a terrible war might have been avoided. If money had been spent as it should have been during early Reconstruction to help the victims of slavery get themselves on their feet, a subsequent century of degrading poverty and segregation among blacks could have been mitigated.

But those opportunities were squandered, and there is no way to get them back. As black economist Walter Williams summarizes, "Slavery was a gross violation of human rights. Justice would demand that slave owners make compensatory reparation payments to slaves. Yet since both slaves and slave owners are no longer with us, compensation is beyond our reach."

Ah, but even with all the parties involved long dead, couldn't we make some sort of cleansing payment that would set things right? The answer is no. The two favorite models for slave reparations—payments to Holocaust victims and interned Japanese-Americans—are utterly different situations, because in those cases the injured parties and the injurers are still alive, and able to make direct restitution, one to another.

Identities have blurred

Meanwhile the identities of "slave" and "slaveholder" have blurred and melted away over the generations to the point where it is now impossible to say who would pay and who would receive in any accounting for slavery. There are plenty of Americans who have members of both groups in their family trees. The vast majority of us have neither—we weren't slaves; we weren't slave masters. Indeed, the majority of today's Americans descend from people who were not even in America when slavery was practiced. And of the people who were here, a much larger number fought against slavery than practiced it.

It gets even messier than that. There were, for instance, approximately 12,000 black freemen living in the Confederacy who themselves owned slaves. Moreover, most of the individuals who came to America as slaves were dispatched into that state by other blacks in Africa. Who owes whom what in these cases?

The villains and the heroes of slavery have evaporated into the misty vapors of our past, and are now impossible to delineate clearly or bring to justice. Trying to pay slave reparations in our current decade would, as one observer puts it, mostly be a case of individuals who were never slaveholders giving money to people who were never slaves. A clear absurdity.

Political scientist Adolph Reed wrote recently in *The Progressive* that the only certain result of a reparations program would be to "produce a lively trade for genealogists, DNA testers, and other such quacks." Even Holocaust reparations—which are much simpler transfers directly to still-living victims—have turned extraordinarily unseemly and debasing. As Gabriel Schoenfeld noted recently in *Commentary*, "In the free-for-all to obtain Holocaust victims as clients . . . competing lawyers from the United States have barnstormed across Europe soliciting clients, publicly castigating each other, and privately maneuvering to oust their adversaries." If you think a subject as somber as slavery wouldn't be exploited (and ultimately decay into grasping, self-serving tawdriness) the second financial opportunism became possible, think again.

American blacks would take little solace from simply being told it's too late for restitution, that practical impossibilities leave reparations for slavery out of reach. But that's not the whole story. The whole truth, which ought to offer black America real peace, is that the U.S. already made a mighty payment for the sin of slavery. It was called the Civil War.

Spoils of war

I first decided to put together a TAE [the *American Enterprise*] issue on this subject [in 1999], when my hometown newspaper ran a Memorial Day ad honoring local men who had been killed in America's wars. The ad listed the names of 85 individuals who had died fighting the Civil War. I later did some research and discovered that the complete total for the three small towns that comprise our local school district was 105 killed.

The thing you need to know to put that figure in perspective is that our rural village contains less than 3,000 people (and was not much different then). The surrounding towns add a couple thousand more. For our little community to have offered up 105 young men to be swallowed by the grave—most all of them between 18 and 29, the records show— was a great sacrifice.

Cazenovia's example was not a bit unusual. In all, more than 620,000 Americans died in the struggle to eliminate slavery. That is more than the number killed in all of our other wars combined. It amounted to a staggering 1.8 percent of our total population in 1865. That would be the equivalent of killing more than 5 million young Americans today.

Rehashing historical offenses is rarely constructive.

The crux that defined and drove this ferocious fratricide was a determination to purge ourselves of slavery. It would be hard to overstate the pain and pathos involved in bringing that decision to its conclusion. President [Abraham] Lincoln's own family is an example: No fewer than seven of his brothers-in-law fought for the Confederacy; two were killed in battle. Yet Lincoln never wavered in doing what was right.

Though they are often now ignored, our nation is peppered with many powerful Civil War memorials. [There] is a monument located down the road from my own home in New York state. Erected by a village of about 5,000 people, it hints at the magnitude of feeling which went into America's struggle to end enforced servitude. Our nation surely did run up a "debt" (as reparations advocates like Randall Robinson . . . like to put it) for allowing black bondage. But that bill was finally paid off, in blood.

The ultimate compensation America offers current residents is a seat in the free-est and richest society yet created by man.

And not only in blood. After tardily recognizing their error, Americans have tried to compensate for the historic harm visited upon African Americans. The massive infusions of money into income support, education, and special programs to benefit blacks that activists like Robinson are now calling for have already been offered up. Economist Walter Williams notes that over the last generation the American people have particularly targeted the black underclass with more than $6.1 trillion in anti-poverty spending. Private and governmental agencies have tried to improve black socioeconomic status with measures ranging from affirmative action to massive philanthropic efforts. And as . . . two essayists, John McWhorter and Deroy Murdock, point out. . ., American blacks have made remarkable progress.

But to the activists, this is not nearly enough. Perhaps there can never be enough done to placate them, because many are driven by an implacable sense of grievance more than a practical desire to see blacks flourish. In his book *The Debt*, Randall Robinson insists that blacks do not like America, and cannot be part of it. It's clear that is his own posture, and he actively urges other African Americans to share it. "You are owed," he tells his audience. "They did this to you.". . .

Creating resentment

This is a poisonous political path. It will be psychologically unhealthy for many blacks, and it is very likely to inspire a nasty backlash among other Americans. In his thorough article on Holocaust reparations (which, again, are far more solidly founded, because the actual victims are still with us) Gabriel Schoenfeld points out that renewed pressure on Europeans over Nazi-era atrocities has unleased on that continent "a tide of anti-Semitic feeling unseen since the pre–World War II era." Aggressive reparations demands have created resentment both among intellectuals and on the streets, in the political arena as well as in social life.

Rehashing historical offenses is rarely constructive—especially since there are so many, extending in all directions and involving all races and groups. Despite the common references to slavery as America's "peculiar institution," the reality is that until the early nineteenth century there was hardly a country on earth without some kind of institutionalized slavery. One of my great-great-great-grandfathers, Mark Staggers, arrived here from England as a "bound boy"—in an indentured servitude which lasted for the rest of his childhood and much of his young adult years. My German ancestors were poor tenant farmers—the European equivalent of sharecroppers—who were repeatedly abused by Napoleon during the very years when U.S. slavery was at its peak.

Human bondage was not an American invention, it was a condition suffered by many people in many places across time. The northern U.S. states that outlawed slavery were among the first governments on the globe to do so. Rather than being some unique American stain, slavery was actually a commonplace sin, and almost six generations have now passed since it was outlawed throughout our land.

And balancing the ugliness of historical slavery in our country is the contemporary reality of enormous freedom and opportunity. Reparations activists will never say it so I will: Despite some harsh imperfections, America has, on the whole, been good to blacks, just as it has been good to other struggling groups who washed up on these shores. As economist Williams writes: "Most black Americans are middle class. And almost every black American's income is higher as a result of being born in the United States than in any country in Africa."

Universal burdens

In the process of taming the wilderness, America's Anglo pioneers suffered heavily from human cruelty, natural disaster, disease, and deprivation. Even the most successful families sacrificed over and over. Of the 56 men who signed the Declaration of Independence to launch America, nine died of wounds or hardship during the Revolutionary War, five were captured or imprisoned, many had wives and children who were killed or imprisoned, 12 had their houses burned to the ground, 17 lost everything they owned, a number died bankrupt and in rags.

Those who followed bore other burdens. The Irish were felled in great numbers building our first canals and railways. Southern Europeans, Asians, Hispanics, and many other immigrants endured long indignities and drudging work helping to civilize a new land. The American society that sprang from the hardships endured by our ancestors now belongs to each of us—very much including blacks, who were some of our earliest arrivals.

There is no perfect accounting in the cosmos, and none of us sitting here in twenty-first-century America really did much to "deserve" the prosperity, pleasure, and long life that our country presently allows (to the great envy of the rest of humanity). We—including those of us who are black—are just lucky to be able to profit from those earlier sacrifices.

The American blessing is available today to every citizen, regardless of how rocky our family's entry into the country. There is no "us" or "them" to give manna, or take it, only a heavily interwoven "we" who share a common interest in the success of our one system. The ultimate compensation America offers current residents is a seat in the free-est and richest society yet created by man. It's the final payment, a gift to one and all.

Organizations to Contact

The editors have compiled the following list of organizations concerned with the issues debated in this book. The descriptions are derived from materials provided by the organizations. All have publications or information available for interested readers. The list was compiled on the date of publication of the present volume; names, addresses, phone and fax numbers, and e-mail addresses may change. Be aware that many organizations take several weeks or longer to respond to inquiries, so allow as much time as possible.

American Anti-Slavery Group (AASG)
198 Tremont St., #421, Boston, MA 02116
(800) 884-0719
e-mail: info@iabolish.com • website: www.iabolish.org

The American Anti-Slavery Group is a grassroots organization dedicated to combating slavery around the world. AASG has helped free more than forty-five thousand slaves since its founding in 1993. The iAbolish web portal serves as AASG's Internet presence and features articles and interviews with activists and freed slaves.

American Civil Liberties Union (ACLU)
132 W. 43rd St., New York, NY 10036
(212) 944-9800 • fax: (212) 869-9065
e-mail: aclu@aclu.org • website: www.aclu.org

The ACLU is a national organization that works to defend Americans' civil rights as guaranteed by the U.S. Constitution. It works to establish equality before the law, regardless of race, color, sexual orientation, or national origin. The ACLU publishes and distributes policy statements and pamphlets on topics such as the death penalty, as well as the semiannual newsletter *Civil Liberties Alert* and the annual *International Civil Liberties Report*.

Amnesty International (AI)
322 8th Ave., New York, NY 10001
(212) 807-8400 • fax: (212) 463-9193 or (212) 627-1451
e-mail: admin-us@aiusa.org • website: www.amnestyusa.org

Amnesty International is a worldwide, independent voluntary organization that works to promote internationally recognized human rights. It also aims to free people detained for their beliefs who have not used or advocated violence, and people imprisoned because of their ethnic origin, sex, language, national or social origin, economic status, and birth or other status. AI seeks to ensure fair and prompt trials for political prisoners and to abolish torture, "disappearances," cruel treatment of prisoners, and executions. Its publications include a quarterly newsletter, *Amnesty Action*, an annual book, *Amnesty International Report*, and documents on a wide variety of human rights issues, such as the death penalty, women's issues, refugees, and prisoners of conscience, as well as various briefing papers and special reports.

Canadian Human Rights Foundation (CHRF)

1425 René-Lévesque Blvd. West, Suite 407, Montreal, Quebec, H3G 1T7 Canada
(514) 954-0382 • fax: (514) 954-0659
e-mail: chrf@chrf.ca
website: www.chrf.ca

The Canadian Human Rights Foundation is a nonprofit, nongovernmental organization dedicated to defending and promoting human rights in Canada and around the world. Its programs educate people on human rights laws and support the development of democratic civil society. The CHRF also holds conferences on human rights issues and issues publications on topics such as refugees and migrant workers, as well as the bilingual newsletter *Speaking About Rights.*

Child Labor Coalition (CLC)

c/o National Consumers League
1701 K St. NW, Suite 1200, Washington, DC 20006
(202) 835-3323 • fax: (202) 835-0747
e-mail: childlabor@nclnet.org • website: www.stopchildlabor.org

The CLC serves as a national network for the exchange of information about child labor. It provides a forum for groups seeking to protect working minors and to end the exploitation of child labor. It works to influence public policy on child labor issues, to protect youths from hazardous work, and to advocate for better enforcement of child labor laws. The CLC publishes advocacy alerts and reports on child labor. The website also offers the *Online Monitor,* an electronic news service that provides domestic and international child labor news.

Human Rights Watch

350 Fifth Ave., 34th Fl., New York, NY 10118-3299
(212) 290-4700 • fax: (212) 736-1300
e-mail: hrwnyc@hrw.org • website: www.hrw.org

Human Rights Watch regularly investigates human rights abuses in more than seventy countries around the world. It promotes civil liberties and defends freedom of thought, due process, and the equal protection of the law. Its goal is to hold governments accountable for human rights violations they commit against individuals because of their political, ethnic, or religious affiliations. It publishes the annual *Human Rights Watch World Report* and reports on human rights in dozens of nations, children's rights, women's rights, and war.

International Campaign for Tibet (ICT)

1825 K St. NW, Suite 520, Washington, DC 20006
(202) 785-1515 • fax: (202) 785-4343
e-mail: info@savetibet.org • website: www.savetibet.org

ICT is a nonpartisan, nonprofit organization dedicated to promoting human rights and democratic freedoms for the people of Tibet. It sponsors fact-finding missions to Tibet, works in conjunction with the UN and U.S. Congress to protect Tibetan culture, and promotes educational and media coverage of human rights issues in Tibet. ICT publishes two newsletters, the *Tibet Press Watch* and the *Tibetan Environment and Development News.*

International Labour Office (ILO)

4 Route des Morillons, CH-1211 Geneva 22, Switzerland
+41.22.799.6111 • fax: +41.22.798.8685
Washington Branch Office: (202) 653-7652 or (202) 653-7687

e-mail: ilo@ilo.org or washington@ilo.org • website: www.ilo.org

The ILO works to promote basic human rights through improved working and living conditions by enhancing opportunities for those who are excluded from meaningful salaried employment. The ILO pioneered such landmarks of industrial society as the eight-hour workday, maternity protection, and workplace safety regulations. It runs the ILO Publications Bureau, which publishes various policy statements and background information on all aspects of employment; among these publications are *World Employment* and *Child Labour: Targeting the Intolerable.*

National Mobilization Against Sweatshops (NMASS)
PO Box 130293, New York, NY 10013-0995
(718) 625-9091 • fax: (718) 625-8950
e-mail: nmass@yahoo.com • website: www.nmass.org

The National Mobilization Against Sweatshops (NMASS) is a grassroots organization dedicated to building a new national labor movement and changing the sweatshop system. NMASS supports the forty-hour workweek, eight-hour workdays, and the fight for a living wage. In addition to the twice-yearly newsletter *Sweatshop Nation*, articles are available on the NMASS website.

United Nations Association of the USA (UNA-USA)
801 Second Ave., 2nd Fl., New York, NY 10017-4706
(212) 907-1300 • fax: (212) 682-9185
e-mail: info@unausa.org • website: www.unausa.org

UNA-USA is the largest grassroots foreign policy organization in the United States and the nation's leading center of policy research on the UN and global issues. It works with the UN to identify better ways in which the international community can use its resources to respond to pressing human needs, such as international terrorism, emergency relief, and human rights. It publishes the quarterly newsletter *The Inter Dependent*, the annual book *A Global Agenda: Issues Before the General Assembly of the United Nations*, and fact sheets on issues such as U.S./UN relations and the International Criminal Court.

Websites

Prevent Genocide International
e-mail: info@preventgenocide.org • website: www.preventgenocide.org

Prevent Genocide International is a nonprofit educational organization that seeks to eliminate genocide. The organization uses the Internet to educate and bring people together, in order to encourage global action. A monthly newsletter *News Monitor* is issued on the website.

Bibliography

Books

Kevin Bales
Disposable People: New Slavery in the Global Economy. Berkeley: University of California Press, 2000.

Cal R. Bombay
Let My People Go: The True Story of Present-Day Persecution and Slavery. Sisters, OR: Multnomah, 1998.

Samuel Cotton
Silent Terror: A Journey into Contemporary African Slavery. West Redding, CT: Writers and Readers, 1999.

Donna J. Guy
White Slavery and Mothers Alive and Dead: The Troubled Meeting of Sex, Gender, Public Health, and Progress in Latin America. London: Bison, 2000.

Amir H. Idris
Sudan's Civil War: Slavery, Race, and Formational Identities. Lewiston, NY: Edwin Mellen, 2001.

Jok Madut Jok
War and Slavery in Sudan. Philadelphia: University of Pennsylvania Press, 2001.

Kamala Kempadoo and Jo Doezema
Global Sex Workers: Rights, Resistance, and Redefinition. New York: Routledge, 1998.

David Kyle and Rey Koslowski
Global Human Smuggling: Comparative Perspectives. Baltimore: Johns Hopkins University Press, 2001.

Binka LeBreton and Desmond Tutu
Trapped: Modern-Day Slavery in the Brazilian Amazon. Bloomfield, CT: Kumarian, 2003.

Rachel Masika
Gender, Trafficking, and Slavery. Boston: Oxfam, 2002.

Gary E. McCuen
Modern Slavery and the Global Economy. Oxfordshire, England: Gem, 1999.

Ozay Mehmet
Towards a Fair Global Labour Market: Avoiding the New Slavery. London: Routledge, 1999.

Michael Rowbotham
The Grip of Death: A Study of Modern Money, Debt Slavery, and Destructive Economics. Oxfordshire, England: Jon Carpenter, 1998.

Jeremy Seabrook
Travels in the Skin Trade: Tourism and the Sex Industry. London: Pluto, 2001.

Dirk Van Zyl Smit and Frieder Duenkel
Prison Labour: Salvation or Slavery? International Perspectives. Hampshire, England: Ashgate, 1999.

Periodicals

Kevin Bales
"The Social Psychology of Modern Slavery: Contrary to Conventional Wisdom, Slavery Has Not Disappeared from the World; Social Scientists Are Trying to Explain Its Persistence," *Scientific American*, April 2002.

M. Cherif Bassiouni   "Sexual Slavery Crosses Moral and National Boundaries," *Chicago Tribune*, February 17, 2002.

Maggie Black   "Wanted: The Right to Refuse," *New Internationalist*, August 2001.

Hillary Rodham   "Talking It Over: Traffickers Turn Women's Dreams into
Clinton   Nightmares," *White House Weekly*, January 24, 2000.

Sarah Downey and   "Slavery's New Face: It May Not Look Like 'Roots,' but
Craig Nelson   Thousands Share the Defining Traits of Slavers Through the Ages: They Are Not Paid and They Cannot Leave," *Newsweek*, December 18, 2000.

Catherine Edwards   "Sex Slave Trade Enters the U.S." *Insight on the News*,
and James Harder   November 27, 2000.

Kim Gilmore   "Slavery and Prison—Understanding the Connections," *Social Justice*, Fall 2000.

Daniel Harr   "The New Slavery Movement," *Social Policy*, Summer 1999.

Charles Jacobs   "Stolen Lives," *World & I*, August 1999.

Richard Lobban   "Slavery in the Sudan Since 1989," *Arab Studies Quarterly*, Spring 2001.

Marcus Mabry   "Out of Bondage: A Group of Christians Attack Slavery by Putting a Price Tag on Freedom; But Does the Practice Stoke the Brutal Trade in Human Life?" *Newsweek International*, May 3, 1999.

John J. Miller   "The Unknown Slavery: In the Muslim World, That Is— and It's Not Over," *National Review*, May 20, 2002.

Elaine Pearson   "Trapped in the Traffic," *New Internationalist*, August 2001.

Alex Perry   "The Shame: As the Gap Between Rich and Poor Grows Wider, Destitute Asians Are Increasingly Selling the Most Valuable Property: Their Children," *Time International*, February 4, 2002.

Alex Perry   "Sold for a Rich Man's Sport," *Time International*, February 4, 2002.

Kimberley Sevcik   "I Was Forced into Slavery in the U.S." *Marie Claire*, September 2002.

E. Benjamin Skinner   "Slavery Is Their Reality," *Newsweek International*, November 18, 2002.

Bakary Tandia   "The Plight of the Black Mauritanians," *Black Renaissance*, Summer/Fall 2001.

Lydio F. Tomasi   "Globalization and Human Trafficking," *Migration World Magazine*, May 2000.

Megan Twohey   "Faith and Feminism Fight Sexual Slavery," *National Journal*, May 20, 2000.

Index